Rosebud's TASTE BUDS

ROSEBUD LAWTON

NEWMAN SPRINGS PUBLISHING
320 Broad Street
Red Bank, NJ 07701

First originally published by Newman Springs Publishing 2022

ISBN 978-1-63881-350-7 (Paperback)
ISBN 978-1-63881-351-4 (Hardcover)
ISBN 978-1-63881-352-1 (Digital)

Printed in the United States of America

Acknowledgments

I would like to thank all of my family and friends for their love and support during the time of writing my book. I want to thank all the people that shared their recipes with me to make my book more complete with all of their delicious recipes.

I want to thank my husband, Jerry, for all of the encouragement and help in making one of my dreams come true—the encouragement of letting me know that my food is delicious and that I should share my recipes with others and for letting me know that I have what it takes to pursue this dream. When we got married, he said his favorite thing about me was my cooking. I wasn't sure how to take it, but it was humorous.

Our daughter Olivia worked at Amazon while pursuing her career of becoming a realtor. One day she called me and said, "Mom, I picked up cookbooks all the time at Amazon, and your recipes are a lot better than most of them. You need to write a cookbook." Of course, usually the food you grow up eating is what you like the best.

All of our children have been encouraging through their excitement and let me know how confident they are in me. They really enjoyed and helped by testing all of the recipes I made.

I want to thank my sister Chery for all of her recipes and interest in my book. She too had so much confidence in me which I guess I never knew that I had. Chery has followed me and encouraged me through the whole process of writing my cookbook. I think that she is just as excited as I am!

My best friend, Val, and I have been friends since we were nine years old. Val has always been a very healthy cook, so for those of you looking for healthy recipes, check out her recipes. Val has never judged me and has always been there for me during difficult times and good times.

My dear late mother-in-law is my true inspiration for my love and passion for cooking. She was truly an amazing person. I would call her for recipes and for directions on how to cook them. I thank her for her patience, belief, and love for me. Sometimes there were recipes that I needed to see how they're done to cook them myself. She would take the time to get the ingredients and have me come over to show me how to prepare them. She was the most loving and kind person I've ever met.

My mother also taught me a lot about cooking. While she was more of a career woman, she still took the time to further my interest in cooking.

I want to thank my niece Jenn and her fiancé, Josh, for always being there when I had an abundant amount of food after cooking my recipes for pictures in my book. They, too, have always been so encouraging.

APPETIZERS

Bacon-Wrapped Pineapple with Jalapeno Jelly

We were camping on the beach in our motor coach with our friends Marty and Joy. We really enjoy their company and I have to say Joy's parents named her right because she truly is a joy! She made these delicious bacon-wrapped sweetened dried pineapple chunks with jalapeño jelly. Another appetizer that goes great on a charcuterie board.

Ingredients:

> 8 sweetened dried pineapple chunks
> 2 thick-sliced bacon strips cut into 8 pieces
> jalapeño jelly

Directions:

1. Preheat the oven to 400 degrees.
2. Wrap the pineapple chunks in the bacon, brush on the jelly, and put a toothpick in them.
3. Place them on a cookie sheet, and bake for 15 minutes.

Again, En-Joy!

Bacon-Wrapped Water Chestnuts

As of yet, I haven't met anyone that doesn't love this recipe. Most people use brown sugar with soy sauce, but I use maple syrup. The maple syrup and bacon are a perfect pair.

Ingredients:

1 can whole water chestnuts, drained
8 slices bacon, cut in half
1/4 cup soy sauce
1/4 cup maple syrup

Directions:

1. Mix soy sauce and maple syrup together in a bowl.
2. Place water chestnuts in the mixture and marinate for 30 minutes.
3. Remove chestnuts from the marinade. Wrap each chestnut in a slice of bacon, and secure it with toothpicks.
4. Discard the marinade.
5. Bake on an ungreased cookie sheet for 15 to 20 minutes, and then broil for a few minutes.
6. Make a mixture of soy sauce and maple syrup for dipping.

Serves many!

Bay Scallops-Stuffed Mushrooms

I make these as appetizers along with my bacon-wrapped water chestnuts. I serve them alone or with toasted baguettes.

Ingredients:

    1 pound bay scallops
    1 pound white mushrooms, stems set aside
    1 tablespoon olive oil
    1/2 teaspoon salt
    1/4 teaspoon pepper
    1 clove garlic, minced
    1 stick of butter, softened
    1 tablespoon fresh chopped parsley
    2 tablespoons Italian bread crumbs

Directions:

1. Preheat the oven to 350 degrees.
2. Wipe off mushrooms with a paper towel.
3. Chop up stems. Sauté in the olive oil 1/2 teaspoon salt and 1/4 teaspoon pepper, and cook until the liquid is absorbed. Set aside.
4. Toss mushroom caps in a small amount of olive oil.
5. In a separate bowl, blend butter, garlic, and parsley.
6. Add cooked stems to the butter mixture.
7. Place one scallop in each mushroom cap.
8. With a teaspoon, stuff the butter mixture on top of each scallop.
9. Sprinkle with Italian bread crumbs, and bake for 20 minutes.

Serve warm!

CHARCUTERIE BOARD

So many times, we have guests, sales meetings, or unexpected guests; and I always have on hand ingredients for a charcuterie board. It's a great appetizer as people like to stand or sit in my kitchen, have a glass of wine, listen to music, and have great conversations. There are various ingredients, but you can use whatever you have or like. I personally like to have cheeses, meats, olives, grapes, apples, baguettes, jams, hummus, and the list can go on. It's really your own recipe because you can put whatever you want on it. I'll put down what I typically like to use.

Ingredients:

> baguette bread, thinly sliced
> 2 tablespoons extra-virgin olive oil
> 1 teaspoon garlic salt
> 1/4 teaspoon black pepper
> mango habanero jam or fig jam
> Maytag bleu cheese
> Sharp cheddar
> 1/2 crisp apple, sliced thinly
> 1/2 pear, sliced thinly
> arugula seasoned with olive oil, garlic, salt, and pepper

Directions:

1. Heat a grill for toasting the baguette.
2. Combine the olive oil, garlic, salt, and pepper in a bowl. Brush it on the sliced baguette.
3. Grill the baguette slices on both sides until there are grill marks on the baguette.
4. Put the grilled baguette on a platter. Spread the jam on it. Put a slice of cheese and a slice of apple or pear topped with the seasoned arugula.

On the platter, put the cheeses of your choice and dried meats like soppressata, genoa salami, pepperoni, and even mortadella. I like to use kalamata olives, olives stuffed with jalapeños, blue cheese, almonds, or whatever you like. Put some hummus, crackers, focaccia, naan, or some roasted red peppers. Use your imagination.

So fun!

Breakfast Charcuterie Board

Sometimes when we have overnight guests, I will put together a breakfast charcuterie platter. People really enjoy it because I put all kinds of food on it and they choose what they like. I like to put fruits, jams, bread, bagel chips, and meats. Actually, if you check out your refrigerator and pantry, you probably have enough items to put on the platter. As with any charcuterie platter, just make it your own.

Suggested ingredients:

small pancakes or waffles
french toast cut into wedges
maple syrup
smoked sausage links
thick-cut bacon
Canadian bacon or ham
hard-boiled eggs, cut in half, or deviled
    eggs
pancetta
prosciutto
cheeses, cheeses, cheeses
cantaloupe
honeydew melon
raspberries
blueberries
strawberries
mulberries

dried fruits
jalapeño and peach jam
specialty jams
flavored butters
brown gourmet mustard with seeds
cream cheese or crème fraîche
caper berries
finely chopped red onion (in its own
    bowl so it doesn't get into the fruit
    or anything sweet)
smoked salmon
bagel chips
baguette, sliced; you can serve it grilled,
    toasted, or just cutup
mini muffins
scones
croissants

Just have fun with it!

Giovanni's Charcuterie Platter

Giovanni is our fifth grandson, and he is a hoot! He loves to work, ride dirt bikes, cook, and he uses his imagination in everything that he does. One day he said, "Mimi, what if you could go to the store and milk a cow? You could get all the milk you want!" We started cooking together before he was three and he is a natural. He's a hard worker that stays on task. We make a salad together, and it's an understanding that you might get tiny pieces of fruits or vegetables or big pieces. He even helps clean up! This is his version of a charcuterie platter.

Ingredients:

> fresh raspberries
> mozzarella string cheese, cut into pieces
> Jell-O with whipped cream
> M&M's
> grapes
> Chicken in a Biskit crackers
> miniature Reese's peanut butter cups with Reese's pieces
> Goldfish crackers

Direction:

> Put it all on a cutting board, and serve!

> I love you, Gio!

Liliana's Charcuterie Board

I went to visit Vinny, Stevi, and Liliana in Utah when my granddaughter turned three. She is my little princess, and she is very funny. She loves to tease people, all in good fun! She makes her own dance videos and loves to sing and play outside. She even made up a show that my daughter Olivia and I were in. While I was there, Stevi and Liliana made up her charcuterie board. She could not believe that she could pick all her favorite foods and put them on a platter in the way she wanted them. This is what she picked, and I am pretty sure most kids would love her charcuterie board.

Ingredients:

   shredded cheese
   hard-boiled eggs
   corn
   Skittles
   macaroni and cheese
   chocolate chips
   pickles
   Goldfish crackers
   Froot Loops with Marshmallows
   grapes
   bananas

Direction:

   Make it your own!

   Thank you, my little princess!

Grilled Chicken Wings

My younger brother David is a great cook. I guess it runs in the family. He is a big sports enthusiast. When my children were young, David gave my son Brian a Shaquille O'Neal basketball card from his college days. He told my son to keep this card because Shaquille was going to be a famous basketball player. He wrote for *Sports Illustrated* for years and also does podcasts. These are my favorite way to eat wings because there isn't any extra grease and they are really easy to make. I serve the chicken wings plain.

Ingredients:

> 12 whole chicken wings
> Lawry's garlic salt
> pepper
> hot wing sauce

Directions:

1. Preheat the grill until 500 degrees.
2. Put the wings on a cookie sheet or anything large enough to spread them out. Sprinkle with garlic salt and pepper.
3. Place the wings on the grill topside down, and grill until there are dark grill marks.
4. Turn them over, reduce the heat to low, and cook for 20 to 30 minutes.

I serve them with celery, carrots, blue cheese dressing, ranch dressing, and hot sauce.

Crab-Stuffed Portobello Mushrooms

I make these for either an appetizer or a side dish. They are creamy and delicious; the mushrooms take on the flavors of all the ingredients.

Ingredients:

    8 portobello mushrooms, stems removed and membranes scraped out
    1 8-ounce package cream cheese softened
    1/2 cup finely chopped green onion
    1/4 cup mayonnaise
    1 teaspoon lemon juice
    1/2 teaspoon Old Bay Seasoning
    dash red pepper
    1 pound crab meat
    1 cup quartered cherry tomatoes
    1/2 grated Swiss cheese
    1/2 bread crumbs

Directions:

1. Preheat the oven to 425 degrees.
2. Beat the cream cheese until smooth. Add the onions, mayonnaise, lemon juice, Old Bay Seasoning, and red pepper.
3. Stir in the crab, tomatoes, and cheese. Fill the mushroom caps.
4. Place in a glass baking dish, sprinkle each mushroom cap with 1 tablespoon of the bread crumbs, and bake for 15 minutes.

Cut them into 4 wedges!

CRANBERRY JALAPENO SALSA

Our oldest daughter, Adrianne, is very funny and we always have such a great time with her and her family. We planned a party for the Alabama-Auburn game. Coming from the North, I never knew how big college football is here. I've even seen fights break out between fans of opposing teams, usually with women. At one of these parties, everyone brought a dish to pass. Adrianne brought this amazing salsa and served it over cream cheese with crackers or chips.

Ingredients:

    12 ounces fresh cranberries (1 bag)
    1/2 cup chopped cilantro
    1 to 2 chopped jalapeños
    4 chopped green onions
    1 cup sugar
    1 8-ounce package cream cheese

Directions:

1. Blend all the ingredients, except the sugar, in a food processor until desired consistency.
2. Add the sugar, and stir until well blended.
3. Refrigerate for at least 2 hours, but it's best overnight.
4. Serve over cream cheese.

Delicious!

Eggplant Appetizer

This is an amazing appetizer if you like eggplant. It has so many flavors going on, each complementing one another. It's essential that you remove all the moisture from the eggplant, or it will turn out mushy; it's called bleeding it out. You might not use all of the flour or bread crumbs, which is fine.

Ingredients:

2 medium firm eggplant, sliced 1/2-inch rounds (make sure that the tops are green)
1 cup flour
1 teaspoon of salt
1/4 teaspoon of pepper
2 cups of Italian bread crumbs

2 eggs
1/4 cup milk
10 thinly sliced prosciutto
10 slices provolone cheese, cut in half
1/4 cup crushed red pepper in oil
vegetable oil

Directions:

1. Wash eggplant, and pat dry.
2. Cut eggplant into 1/2-inch rounds.
3. Lay out paper towels and place the eggplant on them.
4. Salt one side, blot the excess water, flip them over, and do the same.
5. Combine flour, salt, and pepper on a plate.
6. Whisk the eggs and milk together in a shallow bowl.
7. Put bread crumbs on a plate, 1/2 cup at a time.
8. Cover the eggplant with flour on both sides.
9. Dip the eggplant in the egg mixture, and let the extra drip off.
10. Coat the eggplant in the bread crumbs.
11. Heat the oil and fry each piece until golden, place on paper towels, and blot the excess oil.
12. On 1 piece of eggplant, spread a teaspoon of crushed red pepper.
13. One piece of cheese, 1 piece of prosciutto, and another piece of cheese on top of the prosciutto.
14. Top with another piece of eggplant. Continue until all of the eggplant is gone.
15. Heat the oven to 350 degrees.
16. Bake the eggplant until the cheese is melted, and cut into 4 pieces.

Serve with a marinara sauce for dipping!

Hot Wing Sauce

I got this recipe from my stepbrother Mike; he is a chef and created his own hot wing sauce recipe. These wings are always requested for the Super Bowl party. The ingredient that I think makes it the most distinct is the red wine vinegar. I serve them with ranch dressing, blue cheese dressing, carrots, and celery sticks.

Ingredients:

   1/4 cup butter (more butter if you want a milder sauce)
   25-ounce Frank's RedHot Sauce
   2 teaspoons chicken; better than bullion
   2 dashes Worcestershire
   2 dashes tobacco
   1 teaspoon pepper
   1 teaspoon paprika
   1/2 teaspoon garlic powder
   3 teaspoons red wine vinegar

Directions:

   1.   In a skillet, melt the butter over medium heat.
   2.   Whisk in all of the ingredients except the vinegar.
   3.   Bring to a boil and add the vinegar.
   4.   Reduce the heat and let the vinegar boil for 3 minutes.
   5.   Toss the freshly fried wings in the sauce.

Enough for 18 wings!

Pepper Cookies

These pepper cookies are by no means sweet like most pepper cookie recipes. Not all regions in Italy eat these pepper cookies. Our oldest son, Brian, worked for an imported Italian food distributor. It was owned by three men that came from different regions in Italy. One of the bosses loved pepper cookies and would ask my son if I could please make him some. So I made enough for each boss, and two of the bosses were thrilled while the third boss pushed them back across his desk and said to me, "These are not from my region. These cookies are a little tedious but well worth the work. You can eat them like popcorn!" When rolling out the pieces of the dough if it shreds just knead the dough until it is smooth.

Ingredients:

    7 cups flour
    2 tablespoons black pepper
    2 teaspoons salt
    2 tablespoons baking powder
    1 1/2 cups of vegetable oil
    2 cups of white wine

Directions:

    1. Preheat the oven to 350 degrees.
    2. Mix the flour, pepper, salt, and baking powder together in a bowl.
    3. Heat the oil to medium heat and cut it into the flour mixture like pie crust.
    4. Heat the wine to medium heat and add to the mixture.
    5. The dough should be soft.
    6. Roll out a piece 2 inches long by 1/2 inch thick and wrap it around your finger.
    7. Place on an ungreased cookie sheet and bake for 15 to 18 minutes or until they are golden on the bottom.

I also like to serve these with my charcuterie platter. I put a dollop of fig jam on each cookie and top them with a piece of Gorgonzola or blue cheese.

Makes many!

Pizza Rustica, Also Known as Pizza Ripiena

Pizza rustica is also known as pizza ripiena, pizza chiena, or Easter pizza. This recipe doesn't have a tomato sauce, but it is so delicious that you don't need any sauce. Pizza rustica originated in Naples, Italy, which is where my mother-in-law was from. So of course, I was able to get this recipe that we all love so much, even our granddaughter Liliana loves it. It has a dough that doesn't use yeast but uses baking powder instead. There is some chopping of all of the meats. I use my food processor on chop, and it works great. This recipe makes ten loaves, and after baking them, you can freeze them for months. I wrap them in foils and place them in Ziploc freezer bags and thaw them overnight in the refrigerator.

Dough ingredients:

> 9 cups flour
> 1 1/2 cups shortening
> 1 teaspoon salt
> 3 1/2 teaspoons baking powder
> 6 tablespoons sugar
> 5 eggs
> 1 cup warm water

Dough directions:

1. Preheat the oven to 350 degrees.
2. Mix flour, salt, sugar, and baking powder in a large bowl.
3. Cream shortening into the dry ingredients.
4. Beat eggs and water into the flour mixture.
5. Knead the dough together and make a log of it.
6. Slice dough into 10 slices, not going all the way through.
7. Keep the remaining dough covered with a kitchen towel to keep it from drying out.

Filling ingredients:

> 3 pounds ricotta cheese
> 1/2 cup grated Parmesan or Romano cheese
> 1/2 pound pepperoni, finely chopped
> 1/2 pound Genoa salami, finely chopped

1/2 pound prosciutto, finely chopped
1 1/2 pounds baked ham, finely chopped
6 eggs
1/4 cup finely chopped fresh parsley

Filling directions:

1. Mix all the remaining ingredients together.
2. Slice one piece, and with a rolling pin, make a 12-inch circle.
3. Fill the dough lengthwise with 3/4 cup to 1 cup of the filling.
4. Fold the dough over and seal the edges with a fork.
5. Brush the top with an egg wash, and poke the top of the dough with a fork.
6. Bake the pizza on a cookie sheet for 15 to 20 minutes until light golden brown.
7. Slice it into 10 pieces or refrigerate it whole in aluminum foil.

It's supposed to be served cold.

Sausage-Stuffed Portobello Mushrooms

We were at a dinner party at our friends' Jim and Robins. Jim made this delicious mushroom recipe and served it with a wedge salad and steaks. My husband doesn't like mushrooms at all. The way Jim made them disguised the strong mushroom taste. Jerry didn't even realize that he was eating mushrooms.

Ingredients:

   4 large portobello mushroom caps with stems removed
   1 clove garlic, minced
   1/2 pound andouille sausage (you can use any sausage you prefer)
   olive oil
   salt and pepper
   cheese

Directions:

1. Heat a grill either by gas or charcoal.
2. Scrape out membranes from the mushroom caps.
3. Brush the mushroom caps with olive oil, then salt and pepper.
4. Grill the caps until they turn a dark color but not mushy.
5. While the caps are grilling, fry the sausage with the garlic.
6. Stuff the caps with the sausage and top with the cheese.
7. Broil until the cheese is melted and bubbly.

This is so good!

STUFFED DEEP-FRIED AVOCADOS

Believe it or not, the first time I ever had these deep-fried avocados was on a camping trip. Our friend Jim brought a fry baby and made the best way an avocado can be served, in my opinion. It brings out the flavor and creaminess of the delicious avocado. Again my husband hates avocado but loved it cooked this way. After all, I guess everything tastes great when it's deep-fried. Jim made a mixture of either barbecue pork or chicken with a blend of cheeses stuffed it into the avocado halves. He battered it, and then he deep-fried them. Yum!

Ingredients:

2 whole large avocados (cut in half, deseeded, and peeled)
4 ounces softened cream cheese
1/4 cup shredded cheddar cheese
1/4 cup shredded Monterey Jack cheese with jalapeños
1 cup either barbecue shredded chicken or pork
vegetable oil
1 package frying mix

Directions:

1.   Combine all the cheeses and meat together.
2.   Stuff the avocado halves with the cheese and meat mixture.
3.   Put the avocados back together and dip them into the batter.
4.   When the oil is hot enough, put the avocados 1 at a time into the fryer, and cook until golden.
5.   Put them on a plate, and cut each avocado into 4 pieces.

Serves 4!

Tony's Baked Chicken Wings

Tony is our fourth son. He is married to Jaclyn and they have two boys, Tristan and Giovanni. Tony has a tender heart; he loves everyone, and everyone loves him. He has several nicknames that people call him: Tony Montana, Tone Loc, Ton, Anthony, Antonio and, usually, Tony Nasoni! He loves to buy dirt bikes, motorcycles, cars, bikes and then trade them.

Ingredients:

   1 tablespoon baking powder
   1 teaspoon garlic powder
   1 teaspoon salt
   1/2 teaspoon pepper
   1 teaspoon Italian seasoning
   1 tablespoon paprika
   1 dozen chicken wings

Directions:

   1. Preheat the oven to 400 degrees.
   2. Mix all rub ingredients together in a large mixing bowl.
   3. Pat the chicken wings dry.
   4. Line a baking sheet with aluminum foil and put a baking rack on top.
   5. Toss the chicken wings in the rub, put them on the cookie sheet, and bake for 30 minutes.
   6. Flip them and cook for another 10 minutes. Flip them again, and cook them for an additional 10 minutes or until crispy.

Serve with celery and blue cheese!

Watermelon Salad with Scallops and Fennel

When I was growing up, we didn't have seedless watermelon. We used to have a contest on who could spit their watermelon seeds the farthest. The seedless seems juicier than the seeded; it makes a great watermelon salad. This recipe is fairly easy—a combination of cubed watermelon, grilled scallops with a little spiciness, shaved fennel and cucumbers, lemon, extra-virgin olive oil, salt, pepper, and shaved Parmesan to top it off. It's a really nice summer salad, or you can serve it as an appetizer.

Ingredients:

> 12 sea scallops
> 12 pieces cubed watermelon
> Cajun rub
> 1/2 cup thinly shaved fresh fennel (save some of the fronds for presentation)
> 1/2 cup thinly shaved seedless cucumber
> 1/2 cup fresh lemon juice
> 1/2 cup extra-virgin olive oil
> salt and pepper to taste
> shaved Parmesan

Directions:

1. Heat a grill to medium heat and rub the scallops with the Cajun rub.
2. Sear the scallops on both sides, turn down the grill, and cook the scallops to the desired temperature.
3. Assemble the watermelon 4 pieces to a plate. Top with fennel, cucumber, salt, and pepper.
4. Place the scallops (4 scallops to a plate), and drizzle all ingredients with lemon and olive oil.
5. Place the shaved Parmesan on top and garnish with the fennel fronds.

Serves 4!

SIDES

Bacon-Wrapped Green Beans

My husband, Jerry, came up with this recipe to serve with his famous grilled chicken breast. When I first moved to Alabama, this is the meal he made me, and I was really impressed.

Ingredients:

    1 pound fresh green beans, washed and ends cut off
    4 strips of bacon, cut in half
    salt and pepper to taste
    1 1/2 teaspoons avocado or olive oil
    1 teaspoon balsamic glaze

Directions:

1. Preheat the oven to 350 degrees.
2. Blanch green beans in boiling water for 3 minutes.
3. Wrap green beans with bacon in bundles of 6 beans.
4. Bake for 15 minutes or until the bacon is crisp.
5. Place them on a platter. Season them with salt and pepper.
6. Drizzle the bundles with the oil, and glaze.

Serves many!

Barbecue-Baked Beans

One of my dearest friends is Linda from New York. She has a heart of gold and is loved by everyone. We both have five kids, and our kids are as close as she and I are. Every year, we would take our kids camping in Watkins Glen, New York. In the first year, we made potato salad, pasta salad, toss salad, fruit, homemade cookies, and much more. We would kill ourselves making all the food. Much to our chagrin, no one would eat all the food we had slaved over except Linda and me. We finally realized the only food everyone was eating was grilled meat, chips, candy, and drinks. However, Linda would make these amazing barbecue-baked beans, and they were basically our only side. If you like baked beans, this is a sure recipe.

Ingredients:

    1 pound bacon, fried and crumbled
    1 pound ground chuck, fried and grease drained
    1 15-ounce can butter beans drained
    1 15-ounce can kidney beans drained
    1 28-ounce can pork and beans
    1 cup brown sugar
    1 cup ketchup
    1 tablespoon mesquite liquid smoke

Directions:

    1. Preheat the oven to 350 degrees.
    2. Mix all ingredients together, and put them in a baking dish.
    3. Bake for 30 to 40 minutes until bubbly and set.

Serves many!

BLUEBERRY, RASPBERRY, AND CRANBERRY SAUCE

My sister-in-law Gloria made this for a dinner party at our house. It is so delicious that there aren't any leftovers. She needs to double the recipe! It pairs well with turkey.

Ingredients:

> 2 bags fresh cranberries
> 1 cup orange juice
> 1/2 cup brown sugar
> 1/2 cup sugar
> 1/2 cup whiskey
> 1 cup fresh blueberries
> 1/2 cup fresh raspberries

Directions:

1. Put cranberries, orange juice, brown sugar, white sugar, and whiskey in a large saucepan. Bring to a gentle boil over medium heat.
2. Reduce heat and let simmer for 15 minutes.
3. Add the blueberries and raspberries.
4. Cook for another 3–4 minutes.
5. Set aside and cool.
6. Refrigerate in a glass jar.

Serves many!

Bobby's Famous Orzo Salad

Tony and Jaclyn live in a great neighborhood. There are kids running and playing everywhere. It reminds me of when my kids were growing up. No one is clinging to their electronics but just doing what kids need to do. They have this one couple, Karen and Bobby, and they are really cool. One New Year's Eve, they had a block party and everyone brought many different dishes to pass. Bobby made this amazing orzo salad. I couldn't stop eating it, and Jerry said, "Honey, save some for other people."

Ingredients:

> 1 pound orzo
> 4 cups chicken broth
> 3 tablespoons olive oil
> 3 tablespoons red wine or tarragon vinegar
> salt and pepper to taste
> 1 red onion, chopped
> 1 15-ounce can chickpeas
> 1 to 2 cups grape tomatoes, cut in half
> 1/2 cup feta cheese
> 1 teaspoon fresh chopped mint
> 1 teaspoon fresh chopped basil

Directions:

1. Cook the pasta in the chicken broth for 7 to 8 minutes. Drain and cool.
2. In a small bowl, whisk the olive oil, vinegar, salt, and pepper.
3. In a large bowl, put the pasta, onion, tomatoes, chickpeas, and feta.
4. Pour the dressing over the pasta mixture, and toss until everything is coated.
5. Top with basil and mint.

So delicious!

BREAKFAST QUICHE

Christina is Brian's wife, and they have their son, Lorenzo! We were visiting them in New York, and Christina made this delicious breakfast quiche. She served it hot, but the next day I really wanted a piece, so I had it cold and it was just as good.

Ingredients:

1 unbaked pie shell
1/2 cup heavy cream
6 eggs
4 ounces Red Apple Honey Sriracha Gouda cheese, shredded
1 tablespoon olive oil
1/2 red onion, chopped
1/2 red pepper, chopped
1/2 green pepper chopped
2 ounces white wine
1/4 teaspoon salt
1/4 teaspoon pepper
4 strips cooked thick-cut bacon, crumbled
4 breakfast patties, cooked and cut into small chunks
1/2 cup thick-cut ham, cut into small chunks

Directions:

1. Preheat the oven to 350 degrees.
2. In a sauté pan, heat the olive oil to medium heat, and sauté the peppers and onions for 2 minutes.
3. Add the wine. Allow wine to cook off, and season with salt and pepper. Set aside.
4. In a large mixing bowl, combine the heavy cream and eggs using a whisk.
5. Add the rest of the ingredients, including the sautéed vegetables. Pour the mixture into the pie crust.
6. Place the quiche on a baking sheet and bake for 35 to 40 minutes or until a toothpick comes out clean.
7. Allow the quiche to cool enough to cut it into pie-like pieces.

Serves 6 to 8!

CHILI SAUCE

My aunt Connie was one of the sweetest people I have ever met. Now her sister (my grand-mother) was a real spitfire. Aunt Connie was a great cook. She was definitely ahead of her time with healthy cooking. When I was growing up, there was a little sandwich stand called the Pig Shack, and they put chili sauce on top of the meat, which helped complement the pork sandwiches. This recipe is very old, probably fifty years old.

Ingredients:

    25 ripe tomatoes, chopped coarsely
    10 sour apples, chopped coarsely
    2 large green peppers, chopped coarsely
    2 large red peppers, chopped coarsely
    1 head celery, chopped coarsely
    10 medium onions, chopped coarsely
    5 cups brown sugar
    3 cups cider vinegar
    1 rounded teaspoon salt
    1 rounded teaspoon cinnamon
    1 teaspoon nutmeg

Directions:

1. Put all ingredients in a stockpot, bring to a boil, reduce heat, and simmer for 1–1/2 hours.
2. Cool and cover the sauce. Store it in a glass jar in the refrigerator.

COLCANNON

One Sunday, Jerry was making a ham dinner and we were trying to figure out the sides. This recipe is our version of colcannon, which is basically an Irish mashed potato recipe. Of course, Jerry made his famous green beans. We didn't have the traditional ingredients, so we went to our cupboards and refrigerator. We used garlic, white onion, red potatoes, and purple cabbage.

Ingredients:

> 6 red potatoes with skins cut into chunks
> 2 cloves garlic, minced
> 1/2 cup white onion, chopped
> 1 cup shredded purple cabbage
> 4 tablespoons butter
> 1/2 cup chicken broth
> 1/2 cup milk
> 1 teaspoon fennel seed

Directions:

1. In a skillet, melt butter, add the garlic and onion, and sauté for 2 minutes.
2. In a Dutch oven, place potatoes and enough water to cover them.
3. Bring the potatoes to a boil, turn down to a simmer, and cook until tender.
4. Drain, put them back in the pan, add the milk, mash the potatoes, cover, and set aside.
5. Add the cabbage and chicken broth to the skillet. Cook for 10 to 12 minutes longer.
6. Mix the potatoes and cabbage mixture together.
7. Sprinkle the fennel over the colcannon.

Serves 6!

Corn Fritters

My dad was an avid fisherman, hunter, cook, baseball player, tennis player, golfer, and the list goes on. He would take us to Nova Scotia and fly fish for salmon. He would make his own flies for fishing salmon. One year, when we went to Quebec, we stayed in a fishing cabin owned by a fishing guide. He showed us how to trap lobsters, which we did, and cooked them that night!

Sometimes he would come home from a fishing trip with northern pike, bass, or whatever was in season. He even shot a bear once on a hunting excursion with his friend Joe Cutcharelli. My father has since passed, but while we were talking one day, he told me some of his secrets.

At one point, we lived on Skaneateles Lake. He told me that if there was a dead deer or some other animal on the side of the road, he would put it on a tarp in the back of our station wagon. Then he would take it home, tie a buoy to it, put it on the boat, drop it in the water, and let it sink.

Days later, he would take us out fishing, and we would catch a lot of northern pike. We had no idea that he would do that; we just thought that he always knew where the honey hole was. We also had a pond in Barnesville, New York, and he told me that he would hang a string of lights low to the pond so it would attract bugs!

So you are probably wondering why this is a corn fritter recipe. We would have fish fry, and these corn fritters went perfectly with the fish.

Ingredients:

1 cup flour, sifted
1/2 teaspoon salt
1 teaspoon baking powder
2 eggs, beaten
1 tablespoon melted shortening

1/2 cup milk
1 15-ounce can whole kernel corn
oil for frying
powdered sugar

Directions:

1. Sift the flour, salt, and baking powder together.
2. Mix the eggs, milk, and shortening.
3. Fold the dry and wet ingredients together, then add the corn.
4. In a pan, heat oil 1/2 way up until it is at the right temperature for frying.
5. Drop batter by tablespoons into the hot oil.
6. Cook for 2 to 3 minutes or until golden.
7. Drain on paper towels, and sprinkle with powdered sugar.

Serves many!

Endive Salad

My grandmother would always make this salad when she made us a steak dinner. I like to serve it before the meal because the bacon grease is part of the dressing, and it has to be hot. The bacon grease is used to replace the oil that is usually in the salad dressing.

Ingredients:

> 1 head escarole
> 6 slices thick bacon strips cut into 1-inch pieces
> 1/2 cup of red onion, sliced thinly
> 1 tablespoon sugar
> 2/3 cups of white vinegar

Directions:

1. Pull apart leaves, wash thoroughly, and pat dry with paper towels. Make sure to get all the water out because the endive holds water, which will interfere with the dressing.
2. Tear the leaves into bite-size pieces, and put them into a large bowl.
3. Cook the bacon in a nonstick skillet until brown and crisp. Keep it in the pan until needed.
4. Add to the escarole the red onion. Sprinkle it with sugar and vinegar.
5. If the bacon grease has cooled down, heat it and pour it on top of the escarole mixture.
6. Toss it all together, and serve it in separate bowls.

FRIED SQUASH BLOSSOMS

While my kids were growing up, I always had a big garden with a lot of zucchini and yellow squash. I have a friend, Mary, who is Italian and truly an Italian cook. This is her recipe. This is one way to make sure you definitely make full use of your vegetables. My kids would watch for them and excitedly bring them to me.

Ingredients:

> 10 to 12 squash blossoms before they bloom completely, stamens removed
> 2 eggs beaten
> 1 1/2 tablespoons extra-virgin olive oil
> 2/3 cup warm water
> 1/2 teaspoon salt
> 3/4 cup flour
> olive oil for frying

Directions:

1. Wash squash blossoms. Pat dry.
2. Mix together the eggs, olive oil, warm water, and salt.
3. Sprinkle in flour, cover, and set aside for 2 hours in the refrigerator.
4. Heat 1/4 cup of olive oil in a 12-inch skillet. Dip blossom in the batter, making sure to let any extra batter drip off.
5. Fry them while turning them so that they brown on all sides for about 1 minute.
6. Place them on a paper-toweled baking sheet in the oven until you are finished with all of them.
7. Sprinkle with salt.

Serve warm!

Grilled Veggies and Couscous Salad

My sister Chery is amazing at everything, and I mean anything. She is an entrepreneur and has started many of her own businesses. She is also a very health-conscious cook. She started making and selling gluten-free pies, cookies, cakes, and muffins long before it was well-known that a lot of people were gluten intolerant. This is her recipe, and it is delicious. You can also serve this with grilled shrimp or chicken.

Ingredients for the salad dressing:

juice from 1 lemon
1/3 cup wine vinegar (either red or white)
1 clove garlic, minced
1 green onion, chopped finely
2–3 fresh basil leaves

1 tablespoon fresh cilantro
1 tablespoon agave or sugar
1 teaspoon sea salt
ground black pepper according to your taste

Direction:

Blend in a mini blender, and then add 2/3 cup of olive oil

Ingredients for the salad:

1 whole box of couscous
1 package mixed greens
1 eggplant cut up into chunks
1 large sweet onion cut into wedges

2 sweet peppers cut into strips
1–2 zucchini or yellow squash cut into chunks
1 container feta cheese

Directions:

1. Make couscous according to package and allow to cool.
2. Salt eggplant liberally. Place in a colander and allow to drain 1/2 hour.
3. Toss all the vegetables in a small amount of olive oil.
4. Grill vegetables separately so they will cook evenly.
5. On a large platter, layer couscous, mixed greens, grilled vegetables, and feta.
6. Shake the dressing and pour it on top of the salad.

Serves 6–8!

Italian Green Beans

The unique flavor in this green bean recipe is that it takes fresh mint. The red wine vinegar and mint really complement each other. I serve it cold almost like pickled beans. I refrigerate the beans and let them marinate. They are really good at cookouts because the beans don't have to stay warm.

Ingredients:

1 pound fresh green beans with ends cut off
1 teaspoon garlic salt
1/2 teaspoon pepper
1 teaspoon fresh mint, chopped
1/4 cup red wine vinegar
1/4 cup olive oil

Directions:

1. In a saucepan, bring 4 cups of water to a boil. Put the beans in. Blanch for 3 minutes.
2. Let them cool down, and then toss the beans with the rest of the ingredients.

Serve with extra chopped mint!

Italian Mashed Potatoes

These mashed potatoes go great with my Italian meatloaf and corn on the cob. For those of you who like mashed potatoes, this is a nice variation.

Ingredients:

6 medium whole red potatoes, peeled
1 1/2 teaspoons salt
1/4 cup minced yellow onion
1 small head escarole, blanched and cut into small pieces
4 tablespoons butter, softened
1/4 cup heavy cream
1 teaspoon garlic salt
1/4 teaspoon pepper
1/2 cup grated Parmesan or Romano cheese

Directions:

1. In a Dutch oven, put the potatoes in enough water to cover them with 1 1/2 teaspoons of salt. Bring to a boil, and cook until the potatoes are tender.
2. Blanch the escarole for 3 minutes and cut it into small pieces. Set aside and keep warm.
3. Once the potatoes are cooked, mash them with a potato masher, and add the rest of the ingredients.

Serves many!

Italian Potato Salad

This is an Italian version of potato salad; it can be served warm or cold. Rosemary is one of its primary ingredients that is sautéed in olive oil, which really brings out the flavor of the rosemary. Rosemary pairs well with potatoes like my oven-roasted potatoes.

Ingredients:

    5 russet potatoes
    1 roasted green pepper, skinned, deseeded, and cut into pieces
    1 tablespoon fresh rosemary leaves
    2 chopped garlic cloves
    1 tablespoon olive oil plus 1/2 cup olive oil
    1 teaspoon salt
    1 teaspoon pepper

Directions:

1. Place the potatoes whole and unpeeled in a Dutch oven and cover the potatoes with water.
2. Bring to a boil. Cook the potatoes until tender. Drain, remove the skins, and cut them into cubes.
3. While the potatoes are cooking, heat 1 tablespoon of olive oil in a small skillet. Add the rosemary and garlic.
4. Sauté the rosemary and garlic for 1 minute, stirring constantly. Next, add the salt and pepper, and cook for 2 more minutes or until the garlic is light brown.
5. In a mixing bowl, put the potatoes, green pepper, rosemary mixture, and the rest of the olive oil. Coat completely.

Serve warm or cold!

Italian Roasted Potatoes

Of course, this is another delicious recipe from my dear late mother-in-law. She just had a talent for making everything so tasty. These potatoes go great with roasted chicken or steak. Actually, they pair well with any meat. Sometimes I add a couple of sweet potatoes, and the sugar from the sweet potatoes really comes out.

Ingredients:

8 medium-sized potatoes, peeled and cut into wedges lengthwise (6 wedges to a potato)
3 whole cloves garlic
1/4 cup butter
1/4 cup vegetable oil
1 teaspoon salt
1/2 teaspoon pepper
1/2 teaspoon dried rosemary leaves
1/2 teaspoon dried thyme leaves
3 sprigs fresh thyme sprigs
3 fresh sprigs of rosemary

Directions:

1. Preheat the oven to 400 degrees.
2. Place potatoes and garlic in a single layer in a glass baking dish.
3. Drizzle oil over the potatoes and toss to coat.
4. Sprinkle with salt, pepper, rosemary, and thyme.
5. Place the butter and the thyme sprigs on top, the fresh rosemary sprigs, in the middle.
6. Place the potatoes in the oven, and cook for 1 hour, turning occasionally to brown on all sides.

Serves many!

Italian Stuffing

Italian stuffing is my absolute favorite stuffing. It has a little kick to it but is definitely worth trying. It may not sound like stuffing for a traditional turkey dinner, but it really is.

Ingredients:

giblets from a 20-pound turkey
1 cup finely chopped celery
1/2 cup finely chopped onion
1/2 cup butter
1 tablespoon snipped sage or 1 teaspoon ground sage
1/4 teaspoon pepper

1/8 teaspoon salt
4 cups Italian bread crumbs
1 1/3 cups chicken broth
1/2 cup chopped salami
1/2 cup pine nuts
1/2 cup grated Parmesan cheese

Directions:

1. Rinse giblets and set liver aside in the refrigerator.
2. In a small saucepan, add the giblets and enough water to cover them.
3. Bring to a boil and then simmer for 1 hour. Add the liver, and continue to cook for 30 minutes more.
4. Drain and chop the giblets and liver set aside.
5. In the same saucepan, melt the butter. Add the celery and onion, and cook until tender.
6. Stir in giblets, sage, pepper, and salt.
7. In a large bowl, mix the bread crumbs, salami, pine nuts, and cheese.
8. Add the onion mixture and drizzle with enough chicken broth to make the stuffing moist.
9. Place the stuffing in a greased glass bread pan.
10. Bake at 325 degrees for 35 to 40 minutes or until heated through.
11. Take it out of the oven. Let it rest, covered, for 15 minutes.

Cut it into slices, and enjoy!

Italian-Style Beets

Beets are not just healthy for us but they are so delicious! I'm not talking about the ones in a jar or can even though they are good for you and good tasting. They are nothing compared to fresh beets. I had never had fresh beets until my mother-in-law had them with dinner one Sunday. The greens actually have the most benefits as far as nutrition, but you never will get them in a can or jar.

Ingredients:

> 1 bunch any color beets with stems and greens
> 1/2 teaspoon salt
> 1/4 teaspoon pepper
> 1/2 teaspoon fresh minced garlic
> 1 teaspoon minced fresh oregano or 1/4 teaspoon dried oregano
> 1/4 cup wine vinegar
> 1/2 cup avocado or extra-virgin olive oil
> 1 tablespoon olive oil

Directions:

1. Cut the stems off of the beets, and set the stems with the greens aside.
2. Place the whole beets in a saucepan. Cover the beets with water.
3. Cover the beets, bring to a boil, turn the heat down to a simmer, and cook for 30 minutes or until tender.
4. In the meantime, rinse the stems and greens. Dry them off with paper towels.
5. In a sauté pan, heat 1 tablespoon of olive oil. Sauté the garlic for 1 minute, stirring until golden.
6. Add the stems and greens to the pan. Sauté until the stems are tender and the greens are slightly wilted. Set aside.
7. When the beets are tender, drain them and run them under cold water, peeling the skins off.
8. Cut the beets into quarters. Place them in a serving dish with the greens and stems.
9. Season with salt, pepper, oregano, vinegar, and oil.
10. Toss to coat evenly.

This is great as a side dish!

Layered Mixed Vegetable Salad

This salad is really good at barbecues. You can make it ahead and be ahead of the game.

Ingredients:

1 head lettuce, torn into bite-size pieces
1/2 cup chopped red onion
1/2 cup chopped celery
1/2 cup chopped green pepper
10-ounce package green peas, thawed and drained
1 cup mayonnaise
2 tablespoons sugar
2 cups shredded cheddar cheese
10 slices bacon, fried, drained, and crumbled
8-ounce can sliced water chestnuts, drained

Directions:

1. In a large bowl, layer the lettuce and red onion.
2. Spoon 1/2 cup of mayonnaise evenly over the top.
3. Layer celery, green peppers, and peas.
4. Spread the remaining mayonnaise over the top.
5. Sprinkle sugar, cheese, and bacon on top.
6. Cover and refrigerate for at least 8 hours.
7. Add water chestnuts, toss, and serve.

Serves many!

Marinara Sauce

I use this sauce for eggplant parmesan, chicken parmesan, eggplant appetizer, pasta fagioli, or for a quick sauce when there isn't enough time to make a sauce with meat. This is also a good sauce for vegetarians. The taste of this sauce has more of a fresh tomato flavor, and I haven't found anyone that doesn't like it. I found this sauce recipe years ago in a magazine that was interviewing Sophia Loren, and she said that this was her version of a quick sauce.

Ingredients:

> 2 tablespoons extra-virgin olive oil
> 2 cloves garlic, minced
> 1/2 cup yellow onion, minced
> 1 28-ounce can San Marzano Italian whole tomatoes, crushed in a blender (if you can't find San Marzano, make sure you use a high quality tomato)
> 1/2 cup water
> 2 teaspoons salt
> 1/2 teaspoon pepper
> 4 fresh basil leaves

Directions:

1. In a stainless-steel Dutch oven, heat the oil to medium-high heat.
2. Sauté the garlic and onion until translucent. Add the remaining ingredients.
3. Bring to a boil and cook for 15 minutes, stirring occasionally with the lid half on.

That's it!

Potato Salad

When I make potato salad, I don't use any other vegetable than potatoes. I feel as though vegetables such as cucumbers or celery make the salad watery. Especially if you make it a day ahead, the vegetables lose some of their water and crispness. Basically, my formula is that no matter how many potatoes I use, I use the same amount of eggs. In particular, I like to use red potatoes with the skins on.

Ingredients:

    8 medium-sized whole unpeeled red potatoes
    8 large hard-boiled eggs
    1 cup mayonnaise
    1 teaspoon celery seed
    1 tablespoon yellow mustard
    paprika

Directions:

1. In a Dutch oven, put the potatoes in with a teaspoon of salt and cover them with water.
2. Bring them to a boil, and cook them until they are soft but not falling apart.
3. Once your eggs are done, peel them, and let them cool down.
4. Separate the yolks from the whites. In a bowl, mash the yolks really well. Then add the mayonnaise, mustard, celery seed, salt, and pepper. Stir until completely combined.
5. When the potatoes are done, drain them and rinse them with cold water.
6. Cool them in the freezer for 15 to 20 minutes, and then cut them into bite-size pieces.
7. Next, in a large serving bowl, add the egg mixture into the potatoes, and stir together well.
8. Refrigerate for at least 2 hours.

Sprinkle with paprika, and serve!
Serves many!

Quinoa with Fresh Vegetables

This is one of the healthiest recipes that I make, and of course, it is actually one of Val's recipes. It really makes me feel like I'm eating healthy. Val suggests serving it with either grilled chicken or shrimp.

Ingredients:

> 1 cup cooked quinoa
> 1 stalk celery, chopped
> 1/2 cup chopped carrots
> 1/4 cup chopped white onion
> 1/4 cup chopped pepper, color of choice
> 1/4 cup chopped cauliflower
> 1/2 cup black beans or chickpeas
> 1/4 cup chopped cucumber
> salt and pepper to taste
> 1/4 teaspoon dried oregano
> 1/4 cup red wine vinegar
> 1/3 cup either extra-virgin olive oil or avocado oil
> 1/2 cup feta cheese

Directions:

1. In a mixing bowl, add the vegetables, salt, pepper, oregano, vinegar, and oil. Toss to coat all the vegetables.
2. On a large serving platter, put the quinoa, and top it with the vegetable mixture.
3. Sprinkle with the feta cheese.

Serves 4!

Red Quinoa Salad with Fresh Vegetables

Any type of quinoa is very healthy with many nutrients and vitamins. There is a lot of information, so take the time to research quinoa. This recipe is finished with a citrus vinaigrette. It is typically an all-vegetable dish, but grilled shrimp or chicken is great with it. It also takes kale in the recipe; the kale needs to be kneaded to take the bitterness out.

Ingredients:

- 2 cups cooked red quinoa, cooled
- 1 cup cauliflower florets
- 1 cup cooked fresh beets; roasted, cut into cubes
- 2 cups kale (washed, drained, squeezed out, and chopped)
- 1 cup pomegranate seeds
- 1 cup fresh blueberries
- 1 cup pumpkin seeds
- 1 cup cherry tomatoes, cut in half
- 1 4-ounce container feta cheese
- 1/2 cup kalamata olives

Directions:

1. On a large platter, place the quinoa in the middle with the kale spread around.
2. Take all of the ingredients, and arrange them on the sides of the quinoa in their own piles.
3. Drizzle the citrus vinaigrette over everything.
4. Serve immediately or make it ahead and refrigerate it.

Ingredients for the citrus vinaigrette:

- 1 small shallot, finely chopped
- 3/4 cup extra-virgin olive oil
- 1/4 cup white wine vinegar
- 3 tablespoons fresh lemon juice
- 2 tablespoons fresh orange juice
- 1/4 teaspoon finely grated lemon zest
- kosher salt and freshly ground black pepper to taste

Directions for citrus vinaigrette:

1. Combine the first 6 ingredients in a small jar. Season to taste with salt and pepper.
2. Shake to blend and refrigerate.
3. It can be used immediately or refrigerated for a week.
4. Always shake before using.

Serves many!

Rice Pilaf

When I make chicken cordon bleu, I make rice pilaf, broccoli, and a cheese sauce. The cheese sauce adds extra flavor and complements all of the flavors.

Ingredients:

    1 cup uncooked rice
    1/2 cup chopped green onions with tops
    1/2 cup diced green pepper
    1/4 cup sliced mushrooms (optional)
    2 tablespoons butter
    1 1/2 cups chicken broth
    1/2 cup dry white wine
    1 teaspoon salt
    1/4 teaspoon pepper

Directions:

1. Preheat the oven to 375 degrees.
2. Sprinkle uncooked rice in a buttered 8 × 8 baking dish. Set aside.
3. In a large skillet, melt the butter. Sauté the onions, peppers, and mushrooms until tender.
4. Add the chicken broth and the rest of the ingredients to the sautéed vegetables.
5. Bring this mixture to a boil.
6. Pour over the uncooked rice and stir.
7. Cover tightly with foil, and bake in the oven for 25 minutes.
8. Uncover the rice, and fluff with a fork.

Serves 6 to 8!

Salad with a Homemade Salad Dressing

I have always made my own salad dressing, once again something that I learned from my dear mother-in-law. Once you try this, you will see the difference between store-bought and homemade. There are different ways to make the dressing, either whisked together or season the salad with each ingredient. I don't whisk mine first, but either way will work. For a sweeter dressing, you can add 1 tablespoon of agave. Also, use whatever fresh vegetables and fruit you like—cucumber, carrots, onion, celery, peppers, cauliflower, broccoli, blueberries, strawberries, etc. Sometimes I add different cheeses and meats such as pepperoni, salami, ham, turkey, roast beef, tuna fish, chicken, and shrimp. Use your imagination!

Ingredients:

> 6 cups torn lettuce (green leaf, romaine, red leaf, or whatever you prefer)
> freshly chopped vegetables and fruits
> cheeses and meats
> 2 teaspoons garlic salt
> 1 teaspoon pepper
> 1/2 teaspoon dried oregano or 1 teaspoon fresh minced oregano
> 1/4 cup vinegar (whatever kind you prefer, red wine, white wine, or balsamic)
> 1/2 cup olive oil or avocado oil
> 1 tablespoon agave (optional)
> 1 tablespoon balsamic glaze

Directions:

1. Place lettuce in a large salad bowl. Add the vegetables, fruits, cheeses, and meat.
2. Sprinkle all the seasoning and vinegar and oil on the salad. Toss to completely cover the salad.
3. Drizzle on the balsamic glaze for a great presentation.

Serves many!

Sauerkraut Salad

At a family reunion on my husband's side, we had a cookout at Jerry's brother Jessie's house; and traditionally, everyone brings a dish to pass while Jessie grills the meats. My sweet sister-in-law Julie had her parents visiting from New York, and her mother made this delicious salad. It's pretty simple to make, but everyone loves it, and it doesn't have a strong sauerkraut taste to it.

Ingredients:

1 16-ounce bag or jar sauerkraut
1 white onion, chopped
1 pepper, chopped (you can use any color of pepper)
1 16-ounce can kidney beans drained
1 16-ounce can italian green beans drained
1 cup white vinegar
1 cup sugar
2/3 cup vegetable oil
1 teaspoon salt
1 teaspoon pepper
1/2 teaspoon celery seed

Directions:

1. In a bowl, mix the first 5 ingredients.
2. Mix the rest of the ingredients together, and stir them into the vegetables.
3. Refrigerate overnight to allow it to marinate.

Serves many!

Sautéed Kale with Vegetables and Salami

My family likes to eat healthily, but sometimes I have to disguise my ingredients. Our youngest son, Bolton, has not been exposed to a lot of healthy foods. He doesn't even know that his favorite sauce (marinara) is made with olive oil and plum tomatoes. We know that kale is very healthy, but some of my family members (like my husband) don't like kale. With the salami in the mix, it makes it a rich main or side dish. I hope that the vegetables make up for salami.

Ingredients:

  - 1/2 cup red and green pepper, sliced thinly
  - 1/2 cup white onion, sliced thinly
  - 2 cloves garlic, minced
  - 1 pound white mushrooms, sliced (optional)
  - 1 green zucchini, cut into chunks
  - 1 yellow squash, cut into chunks
  - 1 tablespoon olive oil
  - 1 28-ounce can whole plum tomatoes
  - 1/2 cup water
  - 1 teaspoon salt
  - 1/2 teaspoon pepper
  - 1/2 teaspoon oregano
  - 1 pound kale, rinsed, massaged, and cut into bite-size pieces (massaging the kale makes it less bitter)
  - 1/2 pound salami, cut into 8 wedges

Directions:

1. Heat the oil in a cast-iron skillet to medium heat.
2. Sauté the peppers, onion, and garlic for 3 minutes, add the mushrooms, zucchini, yellow squash, and cook for 3 more minutes.
3. Add the tomatoes, water, oregano, salt, and pepper. Simmer for 25 minutes, partly covered.
4. Add the kale and salami, and cook for 5 more minutes.

Serve with grated Romano or Parmesan cheese!

Sautéed Mushrooms, Spinach, and Arugula

I came to realize that mushrooms, arugula, and spinach go together very well. The arugula and the spinach give the mushrooms such a distinct flavor. One year, when we took all our children and grandchildren to the beach, our daughter-in-law Christina would make us breakfast every morning. They had rented a condo, so they had a kitchen. On the last day, Christina was trying to use up the groceries they had bought; and true to the nature of our family, they had bought more than enough. She chopped up onion, red pepper, a leftover potato, and bacon. Then to my surprise, just when the scrambled eggs were almost done, she tossed in spinach and arugula. I was not sure how it would taste, but I knew it would be good because she is an excellent cook. Yes, it was delicious!

Ingredients:

    1 8-ounce package baby portobello mushrooms, sliced
    1 8-ounce package white button mushrooms sliced
    2 garlic cloves, chopped
    1 5-ounce package baby spinach
    1 5-ounce package arugula
    1 tablespoon extra-virgin olive oil
    1 teaspoon salt
    1/2 teaspoon black pepper
    1/4 teaspoon fresh rosemary leaves, chopped
    1/4 teaspoon fresh thyme leaves, chopped

Directions:

1. In a sauté pan, heat the olive oil to medium heat, add the portobello mushrooms and garlic, and sauté for 5 minutes.
2. Remove the portobello mushrooms, and set them aside. Now do the same with the button mushrooms.
3. Add the portobello mushrooms back into the pan. Add the spinach and arugula.
4. Add the seasonings, and cook until the spinach and arugula are just wilted.

Serve with grated Parmesan or Romano cheese!

SHRIMP PASTA SALAD

This is one of my absolute favorite summer salads. Of course, you can serve it any time of the year. This salad has the flavors of roasted shrimp, capers, onion, dill, and more! Take this salad to a cookout, and watch how much people love it. You probably won't have any leftovers.

Ingredients:

1 pound pasta
2 pounds uncooked shrimp, medium to large (deveined and washed)
2 tablespoons olive oil
2 tablespoons fresh orange juice
1 teaspoon salt
1/2 teaspoon pepper
1/4 teaspoon celery seed
1/2 cup minced red onion
1/4 cup nonpareils capers
2 tablespoons fresh chopped dill fronds
2 uncut sprigs of dill fronds for presentation
1 cup mayonnaise
1 16-ounce package frozen or fresh peas

Directions:

1. Heat the oven to 400 degrees.
2. Toss the shrimp with olive oil and salt and pepper them.
3. Place them on a cookie sheet with space between them, and roast them for 6 to 8 minutes or until the shrimp is pink and opaque. Set aside and cool.
4. Cook pasta, drain, and rinse in cold water. Set aside.
5. Put the peas in the boiling water with the pasta for the last 5 minutes.
6. In a large mixing bowl, combine all the ingredients together, and mix completely.
7. Refrigerate for 2 hours.
8. Garnish with uncut dill fronds.

Serves many!

Spanish Potato Salad

Jerry also loves to cook and eat delicious food. He truly is amazing; he is the most motivated person I have ever known. For instance, he could work all day at his career, which is being a great salesman, then mow the lawn, build something, etc. If I too have had a busy day, he still will come in and ask me how I'm doing and ask if he could make dinner for me. Of course, there are times that I would like a break too. He then will go to the grocery store to buy the groceries, cook the food, and do the dishes! This is one of the recipes he came up with. It's not a difficult recipe but really is delicious.

Ingredients:

> 5 medium-sized baked potatoes, baked and cut into chunks
> 1–15 ounce jar of Kraft Cheez Whiz
> ¼ cup sliced green onions (green part only)
> ¼ cup bacon bits
> Salt and pepper to taste

Directions:

1. Heat the Cheez Whiz and toss with the potatoes.
2. Top the potato mixture with the green onions and bacon bits.

Serves 5!

Sweet and Sour Carrots

There seem to be only a few recipes for carrots, so I would like to share this one. It goes well with meatloaf and mashed potatoes. My friend Inger shared it with me. She was originally from Sweden, although I don't think that it is a Swedish recipe.

Ingredients:

    2 slices bacon, cooked and crumbled
    1 medium green pepper, cut into chunks
    3 cups cooked carrots
    1 can tomato soup
    1 tablespoon cider vinegar
    2 tablespoons brown sugar

Directions:

1. Fry bacon in a skillet. Take out of the pan and crumble it.
2. Add green peppers to the bacon grease and sauté until tender.
3. Add the cooked carrots and turn the heat off.
4. In a saucepan, combine the tomato soup, vinegar. Blend together, and bring to a boil.
5. Put the carrots and green pepper in a serving dish. Pour the sauce over them.
6. Sprinkle the bacon bits over the top and serve.

Serves many!

Tortellini Salad

I came up with this recipe when we had unexpected guests for dinner. It's a great time to become inventive. I had some meat to grill, and I was looking for a side to go with it. So I began looking in my cupboards, refrigerator, and freezer. The first thing I came across was frozen tortellini, and I wondered if I could make a salad out of them. With fresh vegetables, cheese, and some pepperoni, I came up with this.

Ingredients:

1 pound frozen or fresh cheese tortellini, cooked according to the package
1/2 cup chopped red pepper
1/2 cup chopped onion
1 clove garlic, minced
1/2 cup fresh broccoli florets
8 ounces shredded cheddar cheese
4 ounces grated Parmesan cheese

4 ounces chopped pepperoni
3 fresh basil leaves, chopped coarsely
1/2 cup extra-virgin olive oil plus 1 tablespoon
1/4 cup balsamic vinegar
1 teaspoon salt
1/4 teaspoon pepper
2 tablespoons balsamic glaze

Directions:

1. After the tortellini is cooked, drain it and rinse with cold water until it is cooled down.
2. In a sauté pan, heat 1 tablespoon of olive oil to medium-high heat. Sauté the peppers, onions, and garlic for 3 minutes.
3. Transfer the mixture to a plate and let it cool down.
4. In a large bowl, mix the tortellini, pepper mixture, broccoli, cheeses, and pepperoni.
5. Stir in the remaining ingredients except for the balsamic glaze, and carefully blend it all together.
6. Drizzle with the balsamic glaze for a great presentation.

Serves 6!

Utica Greens

Utica greens came from Utica, New York. The basic recipe comes from Southern Italy. Utica has taken the recipe to another level of deliciousness! It's excellent as an appetizer or as a side dish.

Ingredients:

    2 bunches escarole, chopped
    1 sweet onion, chopped
    2 minced garlic cloves
    3 tablespoons olive oil
    1 tablespoon chicken base
    1 cup chopped soppressata
    1 teaspoon crushed red hot pepper in oil
    1 cup Italian bread crumbs
    1/2 cup grated Romano cheese

Directions:

1. Sauté escarole, onion, garlic, and chicken base in olive oil for 2 minutes.
2. Add the soppressata and crushed red hot pepper. Sauté for another 2 minutes.
3. Mix the bread crumbs and cheese with the mixture. Combine thoroughly.
4. Put the mixture in a greased baking dish, and broil until the top is browned.

Serves many!

Val's Delicious Pizza Sauce

One night after dinner, we were visiting with some of our friends, and one of them asked me, "What is your favorite food?"

Even before I had a chance to think, Jerry said, "Pizza."

I had to think a minute and I said, "You're right!"

I know I have mentioned many times that I am from Upstate New York where there is a pizza place on every corner—Lupo's, Michelangelo's (Angelo's current restaurant), Brozzetti's, Cortese's Nirchi's, Rossi's, Nick's, Tony's, Counsel's, Roma's, Battaglini's, just to name a few—in a ten-mile radius. Some of them make hot pies, thin crust, thick crust, and various toppings and sauces. So I have had many different kinds and flavors, but are you kidding me, Val! She came up with this pizza sauce that is now my very favorite. The flavors burst in your mouth with the crust and cheeses. My mouth is watering!

Ingredients:

> 1 15-ounce can tomato sauce
> 1 6-ounce can tomato paste
> 1 tablespoon extra-virgin olive oil
> 2 garlic cloves, minced
> 1 teaspoon oregano
> 1 teaspoon Italian seasoning
> 1 teaspoon dried minced onion
> 1/2 teaspoon sugar
> salt and crushed red pepper to taste

Directions:

1. In a small saucepan, heat the oil to medium-high heat. Add the garlic and the seasonings.
2. Sauté for 3 to 4 minutes, stirring constantly. Add the paste, and simmer for 3 minutes.
3. Add the tomato sauce, and simmer for 7 to 8 minutes, stirring occasionally.

That's it!

You can use it for a pizza, stromboli, and even dipping sauce for calamari!

Val's Roasted Brussel Sprouts with Balsamic Glaze

Val is one of my very best friends. We met at nine years old and have been close ever since. She is one of the best cooks I've ever had the pleasure of experiencing her delicious food. Val mainly cooks very healthily with a lot of flavor. I'm not particularly fond of brussels sprouts, probably because when I was a child, my grandmother would boil them and I didn't like the flavor. Val's recipe really brings out a sweet flavor with a slight crispness.

Ingredients:

    1 pound fresh brussels sprouts, cut into quarters
    2 tablespoons olive oil
    1 clove garlic, minced
    2 teaspoons fresh parsley, chopped
    1/2 teaspoon fresh thyme leaves, chopped
    1 tablespoon shallots, chopped
    1 teaspoon salt
    1/4 teaspoon pepper
    balsamic glaze

Directions:

1. Preheat the oven to 400 degrees.
2. In a mixing bowl, whisk together the olive oil, garlic, parsley, thyme, salt, and pepper.
3. Place the brussels sprouts and shallots in the bowl with the mixture and toss to coat.
4. Pour the brussels sprouts onto a cookie sheet and roast for 1 hour, turning occasionally until desired crispness.
5. Place them on a serving platter, and drizzle with balsamic glaze.

Amazing flavor!

Zucchini Casserole

This recipe is so delicious that my grandchildren eat it like pizza! This is one of the recipes from my mother-in-law, and now I have passed it down to my children. Our daughter, Jaclyn, makes it the best. I don't know what she does, but she definitely has put her own touch on it. Actually, anything that Jaclyn puts her mind to, she does it perfectly!

Ingredients:

- 2 medium zucchinis, grated
- 1 yellow onion, chopped
- 2 tablespoons grated Romano or Parmesan cheese
- 1 1/2 cups of sharp cheddar cheese
- 1 teaspoon salt
- 1 teaspoon pepper
- pinch oregano
- 3 eggs
- 1/2 cup vegetable oil
- 1/2 cup Bisquick

Directions:

1. Preheat the oven to 350 degrees.
2. Grease 9 × 13-inch baking dish.
3. Mix all ingredients. Pour into a greased baking dish.
4. Bake for 45 to 50 minutes.
5. Let cool for 5 minutes. Cut into squares.

Serves many!

Zucchini with Cheese and Mushroom Stuffing

We plant a garden every year, and enviably, we have an overrun of zucchini. I decided to look through some of my older recipes, and I came across this one and it is delicious. So if you are like me with a plethora of zucchini, try this out.

Ingredients:

      3 medium zucchinis
      2 tablespoons chopped onion
      1 tablespoon butter
      1 cup shredded provolone cheese
      4 ounces chopped mushrooms
      2 tablespoons flour
      2 tablespoons grated Parmesan cheese
      2 tablespoons sour cream
      3/4 cups of chopped reserved pulp
      1/2 teaspoon salt
      1/2 teaspoon dried basil

Directions:

1. Preheat the oven to 350 degrees.
2. Cut off ends of the zucchini, and slice them in half lengthwise.
3. In a skillet, put the zucchini with 1/3 cup of water. Cover and cook for 5 to 10 minutes or until just crisp.
4. Drain the zucchini, scoop out the pulp, and chop the pulp to 3/4 cups.
5. In a small skillet, cook the onion in the butter until the onion is tender.
6. Add the rest of the ingredients, and stir until the cheese is melted.
7. Lightly fill the zucchini halves, and bake for 20 to 25 minutes in a baking dish.

Serves 6!

MAIN DISHES

Angelo's Beef Braciola

Angelo is a longtime family friend; he is a true entrepreneur and a great chef. He has opened several restaurants, and they have all been successful. When I was a teenager, he had a restaurant in our mall; he had the best pizza. Sometimes we would go to the mall just to have his pizza. Angelo has a heavy Italian accent, so one day I called and asked him how to make his beef braciola, which is the best I've ever had. He said, "You know, a little bit of this and a little bit of that." I was finally able to figure out the measurements. I like to serve it with spaghetti squash, but you can use pasta as well.

Ingredients:

4 thinly sliced top sirloin, pounded down to 1/4 inch
5 garlic cloves, minced
1/4 cup fresh Italian parsley, chopped fine
1 tablespoon crushed hot-red pepper
1/4 cup shredded Parmesan cheese
1/2 cup shredded mozzarella cheese
salt and pepper

1/2 cup Italian bread crumbs
4 tablespoons olive oil
1/2 chopped yellow onion
1   26-ounce carton Pomi Strained Tomatoes (or 28-ounce can of tomato sauce)
2 cups cooked shredded spaghetti squash or 1-pound cooked pasta

Directions:

1. Heat the oven to 350 degrees, and salt and pepper the inside of the meat.
2. Mix the garlic, parsley, Parmesan cheese, mozzarella cheese, red pepper, and 2 tablespoons of olive oil together to make a paste.
3. Spread the mixture on the meat with the grain. Top with the mozzarella cheese.
4. Roll them up and tie the ends with kitchen twine.
5. In a Dutch oven that can go in the oven, heat 1 tablespoon of olive oil to medium-high heat.
6. Salt and pepper the meat and sear it on all sides, starting with the seam side first.
7. In another pan, heat 1 tablespoon olive oil, add the onion, and cook for 2 minutes.
8. Add the tomato sauce, and cook for 5 minutes. Pour on top of the meat.
9. Put the Dutch oven in the oven and cook for 2 hours.
10. Take the braciola out of the oven and place it on a platter with a little sauce on it.
11. Pour the rest of the sauce on the braciola and the pasta or spaghetti squash.

Serve with grated Parmesan cheese!

BEEF STEW

I like to use tricolored potatoes and carrots; it makes the stew healthier and delicious! Everyone loves it, especially in the winter.

Ingredients:

3 to 4 pounds chuck roast
2 tablespoons vegetable oil
1 32-ounce carton beef broth
3 1/2 cups water (enough to cover the roast)
1 cup chopped onion
2 bay leaves
3 celery stalks with leaves, chopped

1 cup flour (more flour might be needed)
1 teaspoon salt
1/2 teaspoon pepper
1 pound small tricolored potatoes, whole and unpeeled
1 pound tricolored carrots
1 tablespoon freshly chopped parsley

Directions:

1. Rinse and pat down the roast.
2. On a plate, mix 1/2 cup flour, salt, and pepper.
3. Coat roast on both sides, and press in using a fork.
4. Heat oil in a Dutch oven until hot.
5. Sear roast on both sides.
6. Add the onion, bay leaves, and celery. Cook and stir until they are both soft.
7. Add the beef broth and two cups of water or enough to cover the roast.
8. Cook with the lid on for 1 1/2 hours.
9. Stir occasionally.
10. Add the potatoes, carrots, parsley, and cook until tender about 20 minutes.
11. In a 2-cup measuring cup, mix the remaining flour and water. Stir until well blended together.
12. Pour the flour mixture in a stream, stirring constantly until it thickens.

Serve with biscuits or bread!

BOLTON'S STEAK NACHOS

Bolton is our youngest son, and he loves baseball. He would like to be a major league player. He faithfully practices every day. If I ever want any statistics about anything to do with baseball, he will know the answers. So watch for the name Bolton Lawton, and if you get his college baseball card, keep it because it's going to be worth a lot of money!

One night, we were going to have leftover steak. We typically make steak sandwiches or stir-fry. Bolton really wanted to have a recipe for my book, so he said, "Why don't we make steak nachos?" This is the recipe that he came up with.

Ingredients:

2 cups leftover steak, cut into tiny pieces
1 cup shredded Monterey or cheddar cheese
salsa
1 cup sour cream
1 cup shredded lettuce
enough Tostitos scoops to fill

Directions:

1. Preheat the oven to 350 degrees.
2. Put the scoops on a baking sheet. Fill the scoops with the meat and cheese.
3. Bake until the cheese is melted. Take them out. Put salsa and lettuce, and top with sour cream.

Also, it's a great appetizer!
Thank you, Bolton. I love you!

Bonnie's Mexican Salad

Bonnie is a longtime friend; she is very kind and helpful to others. I don't know how she does it, but whatever you need, she has on her. For instance, one day, I needed scissors; and without hesitation, she pulled a pair of foldable scissors out of her bra! She loves to garden and cook and can grow her own food from her garden. This is her recipe for a Mexican salad, and it is delicious!

Ingredients:

    1 pound ground beef
    1/2 cup sliced green onions
    2 cups drained kidney beans
    1/2 cup French dressing
    1/2 cup water
    1 tablespoon chili powder
    4 cups shredded lettuce
    1/2 cup chopped red onion
    8 ounces shredded cheddar or Monterey Jack cheese
    4 pita bread

Directions:

1. In a skillet, fry the ground beef drain. Add the water and the green onions. Cook until tender.
2. Stir in the kidney beans, French dressing, and chili powder. Stir well.
3. Simmer to reduce fluids, cool enough to add lettuce, cheese, and red onion.
4. Toss and stuff into the pita bread.

Serves 4!

Braised Pork Roast with Wine-Poached Apples

I like to pair pork with apples; the two complement each other's delicious flavors. I decided, why not cook them together so the flavor in the pork is cooked right into the apples and vice versa? I have worked on this recipe and came to realize that I did not want the apples to be too sweet. I did not want the sweetness of the apple to take over the flavor of the pork. I tried different apples, but I found Granny Smith and Pink Lady apples together made the sauce less sweet.

Ingredients:

2 pounds boneless pork loin roast
1 tablespoon vegetable oil
1/2 cup chopped onion
2 garlic cloves, chopped
1 cup red wine
2 cups water
1/4 cup brown sugar

1 teaspoon salt
1 Granny Smith apple, cut in half with core removed
1 Pink Lady apple, cut in half with core removed
2 tablespoons butter

Directions:

1. Heat the oil in a Dutch oven to medium-hot. Salt and pepper the roast on all sides.
2. Sear the roast on all sides. Add the onion and garlic, stirring until they are tender.
3. Take the roast out, put it on a dish, and keep warm.
4. Add the wine and scrape up any bits in the pan. Next, add the water, brown sugar, and salt.
5. Mix the ingredients until completely blended. Put the roast and apples in the Dutch oven.
6. Bring to a slow boil, and simmer for 30 minutes then turn the roast over.
7. Cook for an additional 45 to 60 minutes, depending on which temperature is preferred.
8. Take the roast and apples out and keep them warm.
9. Add the butter to the sauce, and cook it until it thickens slightly.
10. Slice the roast, put it on the platter with the apples, and drizzle some of the sauce over them.

Serve with extra sauce!

CHICKEN CACCIATORE

Once again, my mother-in-law gave me this recipe and it is easy and delicious. I use chicken legs because they come out juicier. You can use thighs or breasts. Also, I use a cast-iron skillet.

Ingredients:

6 chicken legs
2 tablespoons olive oil
2 cloves garlic, minced
1 red pepper, sliced
1 green pepper, sliced
1 red onion, sliced
1 pound white mushrooms, sliced (optional)

1/2 cup red wine
1 28-ounce can of crushed tomatoes or whole plum tomatoes
1/2 cup of water
2 teaspoons salt
1 teaspoon pepper
1 teaspoon dried oregano

Directions:

1. Heat 1 tablespoon olive oil in a skillet to medium-high heat.
2. Salt and pepper the chicken.
3. Sear chicken on all sides until browned.
4. Remove chicken from pan and keep warm.
5. Add the rest of the olive oil to the skillet.
6. Add the peppers, onion, garlic, and mushrooms.
7. Sauté for 3 minutes, remove, and set aside.
8. Add the red wine and deglaze the pan, scrapping any bits stuck to the pan.
9. Add the tomatoes, water, salt, pepper, and oregano.
10. Bring to a boil, reduce the heat, and let simmer for 15 minutes.
11. Add the chicken and the vegetables, stirring to get the sauce covering the mixture.
12. Cover and cook for 40 minutes, stirring occasionally.

You can serve it with either pasta or crusty bread. Don't forget the Parmesan cheese!

Chicken Cordon Bleu

Chicken cordon bleu is time-consuming and can be difficult to master, making sure that all of the sides of the rolled-up chicken bundles are wrapped tightly. If not, then the delicious cheese can ooze out. I serve mine with a cheese sauce that I make from the leftover Swiss cheese and ham. I like to serve it with rice pilaf and broccoli.

Ingredients:

2 whole boneless chicken breasts, cut in half and pounded down to 1/4 inch
8 thinly sliced pieces Swiss cheese, 4 slices cup into 1/4 inch squares
6 thinly sliced ham, 2 pieces cut up into 1/4 inch squares
4 eggs
1 3/4 cups milk divided by 1 1/2 cups and 1/4 cup
1 teaspoon salt
1/2 teaspoon pepper
2 cups bread crumbs
oil for frying

Directions:

1. Cut 4 of the cheese slices and 4 of the ham slices in half.
2. Put chicken breasts on a cutting board one at a time.
3. Place a piece of the cheese in the center then the ham and top with another piece of ham.
4. Tuck the side of the chicken breast lengthwise, roll up the chicken breast, and secure with the toothpicks.
5. Mix the eggs with the milk, 1/4 teaspoon salt, and 1/4 teaspoon of pepper. Whisk together.
6. Roll the chicken breast in the bread crumbs then the egg and back into the bread crumbs.
7. In a skillet, heat 1/4 cup of oil over medium heat until it is hot. Do not burn the oil.
8. Brown each piece of chicken, making sure that even the ends are browned.
9. Place in the oven at 350 degrees and cook for 30 minutes, uncovered.

Cheese sauce ingredients:

3 tablespoons butter
3 tablespoons flour
1 1/2 cups milk
1 1/2 cups chicken broth
cheese squares and ham squares

Directions:

1. Melt the butter in a saucepan. Incorporate the flour, 1/2 teaspoon salt, and 1/4 teaspoon pepper.
2. Slowly add the milk and chicken broth. Lower the heat and cook for 1 minute, stirring constantly until it thickens and boils.
3. Turn off the burner and add the cheese and ham. Stir until the cheese is melted.

Serves 4!

Chicken Cutlets

When I make chicken cutlets, I like to serve them with my Italian roasted potatoes and a nice tossed salad with my homemade salad dressing. I also serve them with wedges of fresh slices of lemon. The lemon brings out the flavor of the cutlets. Another way to serve the cutlets is to turn them into chicken parmesan.

Ingredients:

> 6 half boneless chicken breasts pounded down to 1/4 inch
> 2 eggs, beaten
> 2 tablespoons milk
> 1 teaspoon salt
> 1/4 teaspoon pepper
> 1 1/2 cups dry Italian bread crumbs
> vegetable oil

Directions:

1. In a bowl, mix together the eggs, milk, salt, and pepper. Add the chicken breast.
2. On a plate, put half of the bread crumbs. Coat 3 of the breast on both sides, pressing the bread crumbs onto the breast. Set aside on another plate.
3. Continue with the rest of the bread crumbs and breasts.
4. Preheat the oven to 250 degrees.
5. In a nonstick sauté pan, heat 1/4 cup of oil to medium heat. When the oil is heated, place 2 to 3 breasts in the pan and brown on both sides.
6. You may need to add more oil for the rest of the breasts.
7. Place the browned cutlets on a cookie sheet with a rack so the oil can drip off and the cutlets are not sitting in the oil.
8. Bake for 20 minutes or until fully cooked.

After they have baked, you can make the cutlets into chicken parmesan simply by spreading your favorite heated tomato sauce, sprinkle with the mozzarella cheese, and return them to the oven until the cheese has melted.

Serves 6!

Chicken Enchiladas

This is my version of chicken enchiladas. I know it isn't authentic Mexican, but everyone loves them. I serve them with yellow rice and black beans sautéed in green peppers and bacon. I serve them right in the baking dish with sides of salsa, sour cream, guacamole, and hot sauce. That way, everyone can season them to their liking.

Enchiladas ingredients:

> 2 boneless, skinless chicken breasts, cooked and shredded
> 1 8-ounce package cream cheese
> 1 bunch green onions, chopped using only the green part
> 1 15-ounce can black beans
> 8 to 10 soft 10-inch flour tortillas
> 2 cups crushed tomatoes
> 1/2 cup sour cream
> 1 teaspoon salt
> 1/2 teaspoon pepper
> 1/2 teaspoon chili powder
> 2 cups shredded Monterey Jack cheese

Black beans ingredients:

> 1 15-ounce can black beans
> 3 slices of bacon
> 1/2 cup chopped green pepper

Enchiladas directions:

1. Preheat the oven to 350 degrees.
2. In a bowl, mix the chicken, cream cheese, and green onions together until blended completely.
3. Place the flour tortillas on a flat surface and spread the refried beans on each tortilla.
4. Divided the chicken mixture, spread it on each tortilla in a rectangle shape 2 inches from the side and near the top.
5. Fold in the sides and then roll the tortillas from top to bottom.
6. Place the tortillas in a greased pan, folded side down.

7. Mix the tomatoes, sour cream, and seasonings. Spread over the top of the enchiladas.
8. Cover with foil and cook for 45 minutes.
9. Uncover and sprinkle with cheese, return the pan to the oven, and cook until the cheese is melted.

Black beans directions:

1. In a skillet, fry the bacon until crisp, drain the grease, and crumble the bacon (save 1 tablespoon of the bacon grease).
2. Sauté the green beans in the skillet with 1 tablespoon of bacon grease for 3 minutes.
3. Add the black beans, and cook, stirring occasionally for 15 minutes.

Guacamole ingredients:

1 avocado, peeled and chopped
1 tomato, chopped
1/2 sweet onion, chopped
2 tablespoons salsa
2 dashes hot sauce

Direction for guacamole:

Mix all ingredients together in a bowl.

Serves 8 to 10!

CHICKEN FLORENTINE A LA MARK

Mark is our second son and he loves to cook. Actually, all of my children love to cook. Mark is so funny and fun to be around. His siblings love to tease him because he takes it so well. This recipe pairs spinach, feta cheese, and lemon together with such flavor you definitely have to have Chardonnay with it. Mark serves it with aioli sauce over homemade fettuccini, but you can use any pasta that you prefer.

Ingredients:

    2 boneless chicken breasts cut in half, pounded down to make 4 cutlets
    2 tablespoons extra-virgin olive oil
    2 chopped garlic cloves
    2 lemons
    2 tablespoons butter
    1 teaspoon salt
    1/4 teaspoon pepper
    1/2 pound fresh cleaned baby spinach
    1/2 pound feta cheese
    1 pound cooked pasta

Directions:

1. In a large sauté pan, heat 2 tablespoons of olive oil to medium heat, and sauté the chopped garlic cloves until light brown.
2. Salt and pepper the chicken breast, add them to the pan 2 at a time, and sauté until browned.
3. Squeeze the juice of one lemon onto the chicken and continue cooking for 10 to 15 minutes or until cooked through.
4. Remove the chicken from the pan, set aside, and keep it warm.
5. Add the butter, salt, and pepper to the pan heat. Stir at low heat for 5 minutes.
6. Place the spinach on a platter, top it with the chicken, and drizzle the drippings over the chicken and spinach.
7. Top with the feta cheese and garnish with lemon slices.

Aioli ingredients:

  2 tablespoons chopped garlic
  3 tablespoons extra-virgin olive oil
  1/2 teaspoon salt
  1/4 teaspoon pepper

Directions:

  1. Heat 2 tablespoons of olive oil in a sauté pan. Add 1 tablespoon of the chopped garlic, and sauté until golden.
  2. Stir in the salt and pepper. Stir to combine all the ingredients.
  3. Pour the mixture over the pasta. Finish with 1 tablespoon of the fresh chopped garlic, and drizzle with remaining olive oil.

Serve with grated Parmesan or Romano cheese!

CHICKEN RIGGIES

This recipe is from Utica, New York, where we lived for nine years when I was growing up. This is so delicious with a mix between a spicy bite to a creamy finish. I know it sounds like a fine wine, but it's really the best way to describe it.

Ingredients:

 2 boneless chicken breasts, grilled and cut into 1-inch chunks
 1 tablespoon oil
 1 teaspoon minced garlic
 1/2 cup yellow onion, chopped
 1 cup mushrooms, sliced
 1 teaspoon kitchen bouquet
 1/2 cup tomato sauce
 3 whole cherry peppers
 1 whole hot cherry pepper
 1/2 cup whole green olives
 1/2 cup whole black olives
 1 teaspoon salt
 1/2 teaspoon pepper
 1 1/2 cups half-and-half
 1 pound cooked rigatoni tossed with 1 tablespoon olive oil

Directions:

1. Heat oil in a Dutch oven on medium-high heat.
2. Sauté the onion and garlic for 2 minutes then add the mushrooms for 3 more minutes.
3. Add the kitchen bouquet, tomato sauce, sweet peppers, hot pepper, green and black olives.
4. Bring to a boil, reduce the heat, and simmer for 5 minutes.
5. Add the chicken and the half-and-half. Stir until heated through.
6. Pour sauce over pasta and mix to blend.

Serve with grated Parmesan or Romano cheese!

Chicken Spiedies with Sausage and Vegetables

One weekend, we were camping in little cottages on Gilbert Lake. We brought enough food for twenty people. There were only ten of us, and six of them were under ten years old. Some of the food items were chicken spiedies and Italian sausage.

One night, my sister-in-law decided to be a little creative with the food that we had; so she took the chicken spiedies, sausage, onions, and peppers and sautéed them in a skillet. She served the mixture over pasta, and it was delicious with all the flavors combined.

Ingredients:

    2 boneless chicken breasts (4 pieces), cut into cubes
    5 hot or sweet Italian sausage links
    1/2 cup dry white wine
    1 red pepper, sliced lengthwise
    1 green pepper, sliced lengthwise
    1 yellow onion, sliced lengthwise
    2 cloves garlic, chopped
    1 teaspoon salt
    1 teaspoon black pepper
    1/2 teaspoon red pepper flakes
    2 tablespoons extra-virgin olive oil
    1 pound pasta

Ingredients for spiedie marinade:

    1/3 cup olive oil
    1/4 cup fresh lemon juice
    1/4 cup white vinegar
    2 cloves garlic, finely chopped
    1 tablespoon dried parsley
    1 tablespoon dried basil
    1/2 teaspoon garlic salt
    1/2 teaspoon salt
    1/2 teaspoon cracked black pepper

Direction for the marinade:

1. Whisk all the ingredients in a large bowl, add the chicken, cover, and refrigerate for 24 hours up to 4 days.

Directions:

1. In a large skillet with a lid, heat 1 teaspoon olive oil to medium heat.
2. Add the whole sausage links, sear them on all sides, turn the heat down to low, cover, and cook for 20 minutes.
3. Transfer the sausage to a plate and cover with foil.
4. Add 1 teaspoon of olive oil to the skillet with the sausage drippings to medium heat.
5. Using a large slotted spoon, add half of the chicken and brown on all sides. Repeat with the rest of the chicken until the chicken is cooked. (Do not keep the marinade.)
6. Transfer the chicken to a plate and cover with foil.
7. Deglaze the skillet with the wine, scrapping up any bits.
8. Add 1 teaspoon olive oil to the skillet. Heat to medium. Add the peppers, garlic, and sauté for 3 minutes, stirring constantly.
8. Add the onions to the peppers and sauté for 2 more minutes.
9. Add the salt, black pepper, and red pepper.
10. On a cutting board, cut the sausage into 1-inch rounds and add to the pan with the chicken.
11. Cover and cook for 10 minutes, stirring occasionally.
12. Pour it onto cooked pasta and drizzle with the remaining olive oil.

Serve with grated Parmesan or Romano cheese!

CHICKEN STUFFING CASSEROLE

If you are looking for a quick and easy dinner, this is one of them. It's definitely not gourmet, but sometimes there isn't always time to cook dinner with a limited amount of time.

Ingredients:

8 ounces Pepperidge Farm herb-crushed stuffing (save 1/4 cup for topping)
2 whole boneless chicken breasts
1 stick butter
2 10 1/2-ounce cans cream of chicken soup
2 10 1/2-ounce cans chicken broth

Directions:

1. Preheat the oven to 350 degrees.
2. Boil chicken in the chicken broth.
3. Melt the butter and then add the stuffing. Set aside.
4. Once the chicken is cooked, take it out and shred it.
5. Add the cream of chicken soup.
6. In a baking dish, layer first half of the stuffing mix, then chicken, and then the soup mixture.
7. Top with the reserved 1/4 cup stuffing.
8. Bake for 45 minutes until it's bubbly.

Serves many!

CORN CHOWDER

My friend Linda gave me this recipe, and it is delightful! With the bacon, cheese, ham, and more, it's not really a recipe if you're on a diet.

Ingredients:

　　4 strips bacon cut into 1-inch pieces
　　1 medium yellow onion, chopped
　　1/2 cup celery stalks with leaves, chopped (the leaves are where the most flavor is)
　　1/2 cup water
　　2 medium potatoes diced
　　1 15-ounce can cream corn
　　1 15-ounce can whole kernel corn
　　1/2 pound of ham steak cup into chunks
　　2 1/2 cups milk
　　2 teaspoons salt
　　1/2 teaspoon pepper
　　2 cups shredded cheddar cheese

Directions:

1. In a Dutch oven, fry the bacon, take it out of the pan, and set it aside.
2. Leave 1 tablespoon of the bacon grease.
3. Sauté the onion and celery until the celery is tender.
4. Add the water and the potatoes. Simmer until the potatoes are tender.
5. Add the milk, ham, corn, bacon, and seasonings.
6. Cook until it is heated through (not to a boil because of the milk).
7. Serve with the cheese on top of each bowl.

Serves many!

CRAB DELIGHT

One year, we went to Nova Scotia; and even as a child, I could see how many more selections of food we had here in the United States. They didn't even know what a pretzel was, and they only had two choices of crackers. We went to this bed-and-breakfast where they also served dinner. While we didn't stay there, we went for dinner one night, and the food was amazing. My mom was able to get one of their recipes: crab delight. All the food was prepared by four little old ladies with ingredients that were available in their area.

Ingredients:

    1/4 cup butter
    1/2 pound mushrooms, sliced
    1/4 cup flour
    1 teaspoon salt
    1/4 teaspoon pepper
    1 1/2 cups milk
    16 ounces jumbo crab meat
    1 teaspoon lemon juice
    1/4 cup bread crumbs

Directions:

1. Preheat the oven to 450 degrees.
2. Sauté the mushrooms in the butter, and cook for 2 minutes.
3. Add the flour, salt, and pepper. Mix until blended.
4. Stir in the milk. Add the crab and the lemon juice.
5. Pour into a casserole dish, top with the bread crumbs, and bake for 20 minutes.

They served it on top of homemade bread!

Easy Asian Chicken

This recipe is from my great-aunt Connie. She was my grandmother's younger sister. She passed it down to my mother, and now we all make it. I do not completely know the exact name of the recipe, but I know that it had the word *Thai* in it. I do not think it is a *Thai* dish, so I asked my sister, and she came up with the name. It really is easy, so it is the perfect name. A roasted chicken from the grocery store is fine or you can roast your own.

Ingredients:

  1 whole cooked chicken, shredded
  1 bunch green onions cut vertically (just the green part)
  1/4 cup sesame oil
  1 tablespoon soy sauce
  1/4 teaspoon sea salt
  1 tablespoon peanut oil
  2 cups cooked rice
  1/2 cup chopped peanuts

Directions:

  1. Put the chicken in a mixing bowl and toss with the sesame oil, soy sauce, and sea salt.
  2. Put the rice on a serving platter, and top it with the chicken.
  3. In a small sauté pan, heat the peanut oil just until hot.
  4. Pour the hot peanut oil on the chicken and rice, and top with the green onions and peanuts.

Serves 4!

Easy Barbecue Short Ribs

These short ribs are easy to make—so delicious and tender. I like to serve them with home-made applesauce. It's a great winter dish because they stay in the oven for two to three hours, and it keeps the kitchen nice and warm. Once they are done, I like to trim some of the fat off.

Ingredients:

1 pound short ribs.
1 yellow onion, chopped
2 cloves of garlic, chopped
1 tablespoon vegetable oil

1 cup barbecue sauce (I like Sweet Baby Ray's)
1 cup water
extra barbecue sauce

Directions:

1. Preheat the oven to 250 degrees.
2. Salt and pepper the ribs on both sides.
3. In a sauté pan, heat the oil. Add the ribs, onion, and garlic.
4. Brown on both sides and transfer to a baking dish.
5. In a 2-cup measuring cup, mix the barbecue sauce and water.
6. Pour the mixture over the ribs, cover with foil, and bake for 2 hours.
7. Remove the foil, spoon the barbecue sauce on the ribs, and cook for 20 minutes.

Applesauce ingredients:

6 apples of your choice, peeled, cored,
   and cut into chunks
1/2 cup packed brown sugar

1/2 cup apple juice
2 tablespoons butter

Directions:

1. In a medium saucepan, add all of the ingredients, bring to a boil, and simmer for 20 to 30 minutes.
2. Stir occasionally if the applesauce becomes dry, and add more apple juice.
3. Once the apples are tender, mash them with a potato. Either leave them chunky or puree them in a blender.

Serve with extra barbecue sauce!

Eggplant Parmesan

This is another amazing recipe from my mother-in-law with a little kick to it. She taught me to always salt the eggplant on paper towels so it can bleed out any excess water. If you skip this step, you could end up with mushy eggplant. Another secret of hers was to spread crushed red pepper on the eggplant. I make the sauce before I start the eggplant and let it simmer.

Ingredients:

2 medium eggplants (make sure that the
    top part of the eggplant is green)
2 eggs
1/4 cup of milk
1 tablespoon salt
1/2 teaspoon black pepper
1 cup of flour

2 cups bread crumbs
1/4 cup of crushed red pepper in oil
    or dried
1/2 cup of either grated Parmesan or
    Romano cheese
8 ounces shredded mozzarella cheese
vegetable oil

Directions:

1. Preheat the oven to 350 degrees.
2. Wash and pat dry the eggplant, slice it into 1/2-inch circles, place them on paper towels, and sprinkle with 1/2 teaspoon of the salt.
3. Flip the eggplant, do the same to the other side, and let the eggplant rest on both sides for 15 minutes.
4. Blot the eggplant with a paper towel to extract any moisture.
5. Place the flour on a plate, add 1/4 teaspoon of the salt, 1/4 teaspoon of pepper, and blend together.
6. Whisk eggs in a shallow bowl with the milk.
7. On another plate, put 1 cup of bread crumbs and reserve the rest to use as needed.
8. Place the eggplant 1 round at a time into the flour and coat both sides with the flour.
9. Next, put the eggplant in the egg mixture and coat both sides. Finally, place each piece of the eggplant into the bread crumbs, pressing the bread crumbs onto the eggplant using a fork.
10. Heat enough of the vegetable oil on medium high to cover the bottom of a 12-inch nonstick sauté pan.

11. Once you have heated the oil, place 4 rounds of the eggplant, brown on both sides, and transfer to a cookie sheet with paper towels.
12. You will have to add more oil as you continue to sauté the eggplant.
13. In a 9 × 13 baking dish, cover the bottom with 1/4 cup of the marinara sauce and place as many rounds of the eggplant in the bottom of the baking dish.
14. Spread more marinara sauce on top of the eggplant, and put another layer of eggplant.
15. Next, take the crushed red pepper, spread it over that set of eggplant, and sprinkle it with either grated Parmesan or Romano cheese.
16. Spread more sauce on top of that. Continue the steps until all of the eggplant is used, and cover with the remaining sauce.
17. Sprinkle with more grated cheese, cover with foil, and bake for 45 minutes.
18. After 45 minutes, turn the oven off, uncover it, put the shredded mozzarella cheese on top, cover it back up with the foil, and put it back into the oven for 15 minutes.
19. Take the eggplant out of the oven and let it rest for 10 minutes.

Marinara sauce ingredients:

1 28-ounce can crushed tomatoes or 1 28-ounce plum tomatoes (puree them in a food processor or blender)	1/4 diced yellow onion (optional)
	1 teaspoon of salt
	1/2 teaspoon of pepper
1 tablespoon of olive oil	3 fresh basil leaves or 1/2 teaspoon of
2 crushed garlic gloves	dried basil

Directions:

1. Heat the oil in a saucepan. Add the onions and garlic, and sauté until the garlic is tender.
2. Next, add the tomatoes, and let them come to a boil. If needed, add 1/4 cup of water.
3. Add the salt, pepper, and basil. Simmer for 30 minutes.

Cut into squares and enjoy!

French Toast

French toast is one of my family's favorite breakfasts. I serve it with scrambled eggs, fried eggs. I have even served it with hard-boiled eggs. I like to use Italian bread, but any bread will work. Giovanni, in particular, loves it. One day, he was riding his dirt bike in our field. He came in and said, "Mimi, I was riding in the field, and I was thinking about that food you made. Can I have more?"

Ingredients:

> 6 slices Italian bread or whatever bread you have
> 4 eggs
> 2 tablespoons milk
> 1 teaspoon vanilla
> 1/2 teaspoon cinnamon
> 2 tablespoons butter
> 2 tablespoons vegetable oil

Directions:

1. Whisk together the eggs, milk, vanilla, and cinnamon.
2. In a skillet, melt the butter, add the oil, and bring to medium-high heat.
3. Dip each piece of the bread one at a time into the egg mixture, making sure to let the excess drip into the bowl.
4. Brown both sides, and serve it with maple syrup.

Serves 6!

Gnocchi

As you can see, a lot of my influence on Italian cooking comes from my mother-in-law. This is her recipe for gnocchi. It may seem a little unconventional, but it is foolproof. Instead of using cooked potatoes, it takes instant potato flakes. They're very easy to make and delicious! Over the years, I have tried to perfect my gnocchi, but either I didn't get the potatoes smooth enough or I had too much flour. One day, my kids said, "Mom, why don't you go back to the way that you use to make gnocchi?" Well, it is a lot less work, and everyone loves them. Serve them with whatever sauce you want like aioli, Bolognese, Alfredo, quick sauce, or Sunday gravy. You get the point.

Ingredients:

> 1-1/4 cup potato flakes
> 3/4 cup hot water
> 2 1/2 cups flour
> 1 egg
> 1 tablespoon salt

Directions:

1. In a glass measuring cup, put the potato flakes, add the water, and stir until they are the consistency of mashed potatoes. Let them cool just so they are no longer hot.
2. On a clean surface, make a circle with flour, crack the egg, and slightly beat the egg.
3. Add the potatoes with the egg and slowly incorporate the flour until you have a soft but not sticky dough.
4. Add more flour if the dough is sticky.
5. Flour the surface that you will be making the gnocchi on.
6. Roll out 6-inch-long pieces, and cut 10 pieces. At this point, you can either keep them as pillows, or you can indent them.
7. In a stockpot, fill it 3/4 of the way up, add the salt, and bring to a rolling boil.
8. Add the gnocchi and once they come to a boil and float to the top, cook them for 1 minute.
9. Drain them, ladle the sauce over them, and mix completely.

Serves 6!
Make sure to serve them with plenty of either grated Parmesan or Romano cheese.

GOULASH

My mother came up with this version of goulash. She knew that her children loved corn and would like anything with corn in it. In those days, corn was considered healthy. I guess I am aging myself.

Ingredients:

　1/2-pound ground chuck
　1/2 yellow onion, chopped
　1 tablespoon vegetable oil
　1 28-ounce can crushed tomatoes or puree
　1/2 teaspoon salt
　1/4 teaspoon pepper
　16-ounce package frozen corn or 1 can whole kernel corn
　1 1/2 cups cooked elbow macaroni

Directions:

1. Heat a Dutch oven over medium heat. Add oil.
2. When the oil is hot, add the ground chuck and onion.
3. Fry the meat until brown and crumbly. Drain and discard the grease. Set aside.
4. Add the tomatoes, salt, and pepper.
5. Bring to a boil and simmer, stirring occasionally for 20 minutes.
6. Add the meat, corn, and macaroni.
7. Heat all the way through, and serve.
8. Serve with grated Parmesan cheese.

Serves 4 to 6!

Grandma's Creamed Onions with Steak Drippings

My grandmother didn't necessarily like to cook. She had a career as a nurse and was very busy. She was always very generous with her love and many gifts for us. One dinner that she was excellent at making was her steak and creamed onions. Grandma would broil porterhouse or New York strip steaks then take the steaks out and use the dripping from the steak to make her creamed onions. She would even prepare them in the bottom part of the broil. It is time-sensitive because the steaks will continue cooking after they are taken out of the broiler.

Ingredients:

    4 porterhouse or New York strip steaks
    6 white onions, sliced
    1 cup butter
    2 tablespoons flour
    1 cup water
    1 teaspoons salt
    1/2 teaspoon white pepper
    drippings from the steaks

Directions:

1. Place the steaks on a plate. Salt and pepper them and set them on the side.
2. In a large skillet, sauté the onions in the butter until they are tender and golden, about 25 minutes.
3. Remove with a slotted spoon and set aside.
4. Broil the steaks in a broiling pan with a bottom to catch the drippings, brown on both sides.
5. Cook the steaks according to the temperature desired.
6. Heat the skillet that cooked the onions and add the steak drippings.
7. Gradually add the flour mixture, bring to a boil, and stir for 2 minutes or until thickened.
8. Put the onions back into the skillet along with the salt and pepper.

Serve on the side or top the steaks with the creamed onions!

GRILLED CHICKEN SALAD

My family loves chicken salad, so I decided to try and grill the chicken, which gives it a unique flavor. I serve it either with baguette, croissants, or pita bread.

Ingredients:

    4 cups cooked chicken tenders cut into 1/2 chunks
    2/3 cup mayonnaise
    3 tablespoons Dijon mustard
    1/2 teaspoon curry
    1/4 teaspoon salt
    3 scallions small quarter-inch pieces
    1/3 cup chopped celery
    1/4 cup toasted almond slices
    1/3 cup raisins
    1/3 cup sliced red or green grapes

Directions:

1. Grill the chicken tenders on both sides until they are fully cooked.
2. Cut up the chicken and allow it to cool.
3. Mix together mayonnaise, mustard, curry, and salt in a large bowl.
4. Add the rest of the ingredients, and make sure that the chicken is completely mixed in.

Serves many!

Grilled Marinated Shrimp, Scallops, and Veggies with a Garlic Olive Oil Mayonnaise

My friend Steve served this as an appetizer at a dinner party, and it is so delicious. Actually, Steve is Val's cousin and Mary's brother ("Mary's Minestrone Soup"). The whole family has great cooks. This recipe calls for homemade mayonnaise made with olive oil. If you like garlic, you will love this recipe especially because the garlic is raw. I either make this as a side dish with rice pilaf or as an appetizer. Either way, it is amazing especially because of the garlic mayonnaise.

Ingredients:

> 1 pound raw peeled and deveined shrimp
> 1 pound raw sea scallops
> 1/2 pounds cherry tomatoes
> 2 peppers, any color (I prefer red)
> 1 pound whole mushrooms

Marinade:

> 1/3 cup extra-virgin olive oil
> 1/4 lemon juice
> 1/4 cup white vinegar
> 2 garlic cloves, minced
> 1 tablespoon fresh parsley leaves, chopped
> 1 tablespoon fresh basil, chopped
> 1/2 teaspoon dried oregano
> 1 teaspoon salt
> 1/2 teaspoon black pepper

Directions for the marinade:

1. Combine all the marinade ingredients.
2. Put the shrimp, scallops, and vegetables in their own container. Divide the marinade between them.
3. Marinate for 24 hours.

Mayonnaise:

    1 large egg
    2 medium cloves garlic, minced
    1 tablespoon fresh lemon juice
    1 hard-cooked egg yolk
    1 teaspoon Dijon mustard
    1/4 teaspoon pepper
    1/4 teaspoon salt
    2 cups olive oil

Directions for the mayonnaise:

1. Blend the first 7 ingredients in a food processor.
2. With the food processor going gradually, add the olive oil to the mixture in a thin stream.
3. Blend until it is smooth and thick. You may not need all of the olive oil.
4. Prepare the mayonnaise 2 days in advance.

Let's put it all together!

1. Skewer all the marinated ingredients separately because they cook for different amounts of time.
2. Grill on both sides until everything is done.
3. Line a platter with romaine lettuce and put a bowl of mayonnaise in the center.
4. Either take the food off the skewers or serve on the skewers.

Serves 4!

Ham and Fruit Kebabs with a Peach Jalapeno Glaze

These are really fun and can either be served as an appetizer or main dish over rice pilaf. The ham pairs well with the grilled fruits and vegetables. Most vegetables or fruit will work for the kebabs.

Ingredients:

- 2 to 2 1/2 pounds boneless ham cut into 1 1/2 inch cubes
- 2 medium zucchinis cut into thick slices
- 1 cup pineapple chunks (use either fresh or canned)
- 2 peaches, skinned and cut into chunks
- 1 package whole white mushrooms
- 1 green pepper cut into chunks
- 1 cup peach jam
- 2 jalapeños, sliced thin without the seeds

Directions:

1. Skewer the ham, vegetables, and fruit according to their kind and place on a cookie sheet.
2. In a small saucepan, combine the peach jam and jalapeños and heat just until heated through.
3. Pour the peach glaze over the skewers and let set for 30 minutes.
4. Grill all the skewers until grill marks are on all sides.

Serves 6!

Italian Wedding Soup with Meatballs and Stracciatella

This is the soup in which we will be using the leftover roasted chicken. An uncooked chicken can be used as well but the cooking time will be longer. Italian wedding soup got its name from the marriage of the vegetables and meat, not necessarily served at weddings. The stracciatella, which is basically Italian egg drop soup, and the spinach add so much flavor. I serve it with a family dinner for a starter or by itself as a meal.

Ingredients:

> 1 leftover chicken carcass or a 3-pound whole uncooked chicken
> enough water to cover the chicken
> 2 tablespoons chicken base
> 2 whole celery stalks with leaves chopped (the leaves have great flavor and many nutrients)
> 1 whole yellow onion, chopped
> 2 whole cloves garlic
> 2 large carrots, peeled and sliced crosswise
> 6 ounces baby spinach leaves

Meatballs:

> 1 pound ground chuck
> 1/2 cup of bread crumbs
> 1 egg beaten
> 1 tablespoon milk
> 1/4 teaspoon garlic powder
> 1/4 teaspoon black pepper

Stracciatella:

> 2 large eggs
> 2 tablespoons grated Parmesan
> 2 tablespoons chopped parsley

Directions for the soup:

1. Put the chicken, water, and chicken base in the pot.
2. Bring the broth to a boil, reduce heat, and simmer for 1 hour.
3. Take the carcass out, and pick all the meat off the bones.
4. Strain the broth in a colander to get all the little tiny bones out.
5. Return the broth to the pot. Add the onion, celery, and garlic. Simmer for 30 minutes.
6. Add the carrots, and cook for 20 more minutes, then add the spinach.

Directions for the meatballs:

1. In a bowl, mix all of the ingredients and roll into 2-inch balls.
2. Place them on an ungreased cookie sheet and bake for 15 to 20 minutes or until they are browned on the outside.
3. Remove from the oven, let them rest for 5 minutes, and add them when the carrots are added.

Directions for stracciatella:

1. Bring the soup to medium-high heat.
2. In a bowl, whisk all ingredients to blend together. Reduce the heat to medium low.
3. Stir the broth in a circular motion, and gradually drizzle the egg mixture into the moving broth.
4. Stir gently with a fork to form thin strands of the egg for 1 minute.

Serve with grated Parmesan or Romano cheese!

Lasagna

When I make lasagna, I make my own pasta. It really makes a difference. I have a KitchenAid stand-up mixer with an attachment to roll out the pasta, but you can use a hand-cranked pasta machine. The velvetiness of the pasta takes the lasagna to another level. Store-bought lasagna noodles will work as well. You won't need to boil the homemade lasagna noodles; you don't even have to cut them into strips because when the lasagna is done, you cut the lasagna into squares.

Lasagna ingredients:

> basic pasta dough × 3 (recipe will follow)
> 1 pound ground Italian sausage
> 1 1/2 pounds ground chuck
> 1 tablespoon vegetable oil
> 1/2 cup chopped yellow onion
> 2 cloves garlic, chopped
> 1 28-ounce can crushed tomatoes
> 1 28-ounce can tomato puree
> 1 tablespoon salt
> 1/2 teaspoon pepper
> 4 whole basil leaves
> 3 16-ounce containers ricotta cheese
> 3 cups shredded mozzarella cheese
> 1/2 cup grated Parmesan cheese
> 2 eggs

Directions:

1. In a Dutch oven, heat the oil, add the onions, garlic, and sauté until the onion is soft.
2. Add the sausage and ground chuck. Cook until the meat is done.
3. Add the crushed tomatoes, puree, salt, pepper, and basil. Bring to a boil, and cook for 3 minutes.
4. Turn down the heat to a simmer and cook for 30 minutes.
5. In a large bowl, mix the ricotta cheese, eggs, and parsley. Set aside.
6. Ladder some of the sauce mixture in a 9 × 14-inch pan, 4 inches deep.

7. Place a single layer of pasta. Spread some of the ricotta, mozzarella, and grated cheese.
8. Ladle some of the meat mixture on top of the cheese. Continue these steps until all the ingredients are used.
9. Top with a single layer of the pasta, and top it with the sauce without the meat.
10. Cover with foil and bake at 350 for 45 minutes. Remove the foil and continue cooking for 15 minutes, take the lasagna out of the oven and top with the mozzarella cheese and loosely cover with the foil until the cheese is melted.

Let the lasagna rest for 15 minutes before serving it.

Basic pasta dough ingredients:

1 egg
3/4 cup of flour

Directions:

1. Make a well or circle of the flours, break the egg, beat the egg lightly, and start incorporating the flour until mixed thoroughly.
2. Knead for 5 minutes, wrap in plastic, and refrigerate for 2 hours up to overnight.
3. Roll out the dough to 1/8 of an inch.

Serve with extra sauce and grated cheese!

Lentil Soup with Kielbasa

This is a hearty soup and is excellent for watching Sunday football. Serve it with corn bread or crusty bread. My sister Chery actually gave me this recipe, and both our families love it.

Ingredients:

1 package dry lentils, rinsed and drained
2 cups cold water
1 16-ounce can crushed tomatoes
7 slices bacon
1 yellow onion, chopped
2 celery stalks, chopped
4 carrots, sliced
salt and pepper to taste
1 bay leaf
1 pound kielbasa, cut in rounds

Directions:

1. After you have thoroughly rinsed the lentils, boil them in the water for 15 minutes.
2. In the meantime, cook the bacon and chop it up.
3. Leave 1 tablespoon of the bacon grease in the pan and sauté the onions.
4. Add the tomatoes, bacon, onion, celery, and carrots.
5. Boil for 30 minutes.
6. Add the kielbasa, salt, pepper, and bay leaf.
7. Simmer for 1 hour and serve.

Serves many!
Thanks, sis!

Lorenzo's Sloppy Joe Mac and Cheese with Bacon

Our grandson Lorenzo is such a sweetheart. I guess I'm partial, but he has such a kind heart. I was talking to our son Brian about giving me one of his signature recipes, chicken marsala, and Lorenzo must have been listening. When I talk to people about my cookbook inevitably, they say, "Oh, can I give you a recipe to put in your book?"

I say, "Of course, I would love that."

Now it's another thing to actually get the recipe from them; everyone is so busy. One day, Lorenzo sent me a recipe that he made up himself, even with a picture. It really touched my heart! Our son Brian and his wife, Christina, eat very healthily; so even though this recipe has macaroni and cheese in it, it is homemade and not from a box. He specifically uses Kerrygold cheddar cheese, which is sharp. He said that you could use a combination of mild and sharp. There may not be Kerrygold in your area, so use whatever is available. I can't say that it is completely healthy, but coming from a thirteen-year-old, it's delicious!

Ingredients:

1 1/2 cups elbow macaroni, uncooked
1/4 cup butter
1/4 cup flour
1/4 teaspoon salt
1 1/3 cups whole milk
1 cup shredded Kerrygold cheddar cheese

1 pound ground beef
1 package sloppy joe mix with needed ingredients according to the directions
4 strips bacon, cooked and crumbled

Directions:

1. Cook the macaroni according to the package, and set it aside.
2. In a saucepan on medium-low heat, melt the butter, add the flour, and whisk until smooth.
3. Gradually add the milk, making sure that you constantly whisk the mixture.
4. Eventually the mixture will start to bubble. Turn off the heat and add the salt and cheese.
5. Make sure that all of the cheese is melted and completely folded together.
6. Add the cooked macaroni, and stir to coat completely. Set aside.
7. In a sauté pan, fry the ground beef, drain, and follow the directions on the package.
8. Pour the sloppy joe mix in the macaroni and cheese, then mix completely.
9. Pour the entire mixture into a serving dish, and top with the bacon.

Just fantastic!
I love you, Lorenzo!

Mary's Minestrone Soup

One of my dearest friends Mary was an amazing cook and one of the kindest persons you could ever meet. Unfortunately, Mary passed away from cancer and is dearly missed. She made recipes her own by adding a little bit of this and a little bit of that. She would serve the soup with pumpernickel bread finished with honey butter.

Ingredients:

1 pound boneless chuck roast cut into 1/2-inch chunks
2 yellow onions, chopped
2 cloves garlic, minced
1 teaspoon vegetable oil
4 carrots, thinly sliced
1 stalk celery, thinly sliced
one 16-ounce can stew tomatoes, undrained and chopped
1 cup chopped cabbage
2 1/2 cups of chicken broth
2 1/2 cups of beef broth
2 cups water
1 bay leaf
1 teaspoon black pepper
2 teaspoons salt
1 can chickpeas, drained
1 can red kidney beans, drained
1 1/2 cups of fresh green beans, cut into 1-inch pieces
1 10-ounce package frozen peas
1 cup spaghetti, broken into small pieces

Directions:

1. In a Dutch oven, heat the oil.
2. Add the beef onions, garlic, and fry for 10 minutes.
3. Add the next 10 ingredients.
4. Cover the Dutch oven and simmer for 2 hours or until the meat is tender.
5. Add the remaining ingredients and simmer for an additional 45 minutes.

Pumpernickel bread with honey butter ingredients:

     8 slices pumpernickel bread
     1 stick softened butter
     2 tablespoons honey
     1/4 cup finely chopped raisins

Directions:

1. Beat together butter, honey, and raisins until blended.
2. Spread butter mixture on the pumpernickel bread.
3. Broil the bread for 1 minute or until the butter is melted.

Serves many!

Pasta Fagioli

Pasta fagioli is another one of those Italian dishes that varies from region to region in Italy. This recipe is from my dear mother-in-law, who was from Naples. I like this version best, but they are all delicious. Some versions are thicker, quicker, and are cooked with sausage; but this one is more like a soup with so many flavors! A lot of times, she would have a ham dinner and take the remainder of the ham hock and make pasta fagioli. She was the queen of reinventing leftovers.

Ingredients:

1 bag dry great northern beans
2 bay leaves
1 1/2 to 2 pounds ham hock
2 stalks of celery with leaves, chopped
1 tablespoon oil
2 garlic cloves, chopped

1 medium yellow onion, chopped
1 28-ounce can of crushed tomatoes
2 teaspoons salt
1 teaspoon pepper
1 pound ditalini or orecchiette pasta
grated Parmesan or Romano cheese

Directions:

1. Soak the beans overnight in enough water to cover them.
2. After the beans have soaked overnight, rinse and drain them.
3. Put the beans in a Dutch oven with the ham, celery, bay leaves and enough water to cover the ham.
4. Bring to a boil and cook for 30 minutes, stirring with a wooden spoon.
5. In the meantime, heat the oil and sauté the onion and garlic for 3 to 5 minutes.
6. Add the tomatoes to the pan with the salt and pepper, and cook for 20 minutes, stirring occasionally.
7. Add the sauce into the Dutch oven with the beans and cook for 30 more minutes.
8. Take out the ham hock, get all the meat off the bone, cut it into chunks, and add it to the Dutch oven.
9. Cook the pasta, drain it, and add it to the Dutch oven.
10. Season with salt and pepper.

Serve with the grated cheese!

Pasta Primavera

For those of you that don't really want to eat meat, this is a perfect alternative. Make sure that you cook the pasta al dente because the vegetables have a lot of liquid.

Ingredients:

2 tablespoons extra-virgin olive oil
1 cup sliced mushrooms
2 cloves garlic, minced
1 yellow onion, chopped
2 carrots, thinly sliced
1 red pepper, thinly sliced
1 cup spinach, cut into strips
1 1/4 cups vegetable broth
1 tablespoon cornstarch
2 tablespoons fresh chopped parsley
1/4 teaspoon salt
1/4 teaspoon pepper
1/4 cup grated Parmesan cheese
1 pound linguini

Directions:

1. In a large skillet, heat the oil.
2. Add the mushrooms, garlic, and onions. Sauté for 5 minutes.
3. Add the carrots, peppers, and spinach. Cook for 5 minutes longer, then add the tomatoes.
4. Mix together the cornstarch, vegetable broth, parsley, salt, and pepper.
5. Stir into the pan, bring to a boil, and cook on low until thickened.
6. Stir in the Parmesan cheese.
7. Pour over the cooked pasta and mix thoroughly.

Serve with grated Parmesan cheese!

Pesto Rigatoni with Grilled Chicken and Tomatoes

This is another one of Vinny's recipes. He loves incorporating pesto into his recipes. He also has artichokes in this recipe that are grilled and packed in oil. He sends me pictures of different food he makes, and I tell him, "I want that recipe."

Ingredients:

1 pound boneless chicken breast, seasoned with *pinch*
1 15-ounce jar grilled artichokes, packed in oil
2 cups grape tomatoes, cut in half
4 tablespoons green pesto
1 garlic clove, minced
1 pound cooked rigatoni
crushed red pepper to taste
Parmesan cheese

Directions:

1. Grill chicken, and cut it into bite-size pieces.
2. In a bowl, mix the pesto, garlic, and tomatoes until well blended.
3. Add the pasta and the chicken to the bowl, and toss to coat evenly.
4. Sprinkle with red pepper and cheese.

Serve with extra Parmesan cheese!

POLPETTONE

Well, my sister did it again and gave me a delicious recipe. She got it from her dear friend Maria. Maria's parents are from Sicily. Sicily is in Italy and Sicilians are Italian, but not all Italians are Sicilian. Sicilian food gets more of its influence from Spanish, Arab, and Greek cooking. I realized how actually spoiled we are in America; Italians cook with whatever is most bountiful in their region. For instance, if you live in Southern Italy, you cook more with fish and vegetables while Northern Italy is hilly. They cook more goat and they also make so many different variations from goat's and sheep's milk. This is called polpettone or stuffed Sicilian meatloaf.

Ingredients:

1 pound ground beef
1 pound ground pork or beef
1/2 cup Italian bread crumbs
1/2 cup grated Parmesan cheese
1/2 cup milk
2 slices stale bread
2 eggs, beaten
1 teaspoon chopped Italian parsley
1/2 teaspoon garlic powder

1 teaspoon salt
1/4 teaspoon pepper
1/2 pound prosciutto
1/2 pound sliced mozzarella or provolone cheese
1 roasted red pepper, sliced
6 ounces fresh spinach
3 to 4 hard-boiled eggs

Directions:

1. In a large mixing bowl, combine the first 10 ingredients.
2. With your hands, mix until all the ingredients are completely combined.
3. Lay out a large strip of plastic, wrap on the counter, and spray it with olive oil.
4. Spread the meat mixture on it flatly, and square off the edges.
5. Layer the spinach, prosciutto, cheese, and red pepper strips. Top with the eggs.
6. Using the plastic wrap, gently roll the meat together, lengthwise. Pull off the plastic wrap and seal the meat together with your hands.
7. Either bake the meatloaf or wrap it up tightly and refrigerate for 1 day.
8. Bake at 375 degrees until sizzling and the cheese in the middle starts to leak out a bit.
9. Take the meatloaf out of the oven. Let it rest for 10 minutes, and slice it up.

Serve with a marinara sauce and grated Parmesan cheese!

Portuguese Soup

This is a great Sunday dish; it's called a soup, but it's really more like a stew. There are many different flavors from all the different ingredients.

Ingredients:

  1 bone-in ham shank
  4 quarts water
  8-ounce can tomato sauce
  1 onion, chopped
  2 whole cloves garlic
  1 pound each dry white kidney beans and red kidney beans
  2 teaspoons salt
  1 teaspoon pepper
  2 cups cubed potatoes
  1 1/2 cups sliced carrots
  6 cups cabbage, chopped
  8 ounces uncooked spaghetti

Directions:

  1. In a stockpot, put the ham, water, tomato sauce, onion, garlic, kidney beans, salt, and pepper.
  2. Bring to a boil, turn it down, and simmer for 5 hours.
  3. Remove the ham, take the meat off the bone, and cut it into chunks.
  4. Add the carrots, potatoes, cabbage, and spaghetti. Cook for 45 minutes longer.

Serves many!

Puttanesca Sauce

They are many different theories about how puttanesca sauce got its name. Some people believe that one night, a restaurant owner had a bunch of guests come in late. He didn't have any real ingredients to make a meal, so he put together what he had. The other theory is that ladies of the evening would make this easy, unique, and delicious sauce to lure clients in. Either way, it is delicious!

Ingredients:

  3 tablespoons olive oil
  8 tablespoons butter
  1 clove garlic, chopped
  8 anchovy filets, minced
  1 1/2 cups Italian peeled tomatoes
  1 teaspoon black pepper
  1/4 cup capers
  3/4 cup black olives, cut in half
  1 tablespoon fresh chopped parsley
  pinch of oregano
  2 fresh basil leaves
  1/2 cup grated Romano or Parmesan cheese
  1 pound capellini

Directions:

1. In a large sauté pan, heat the oil and 4 tablespoons of butter.
2. Add the garlic and anchovies and cook it quickly without browning the garlic.
3. Add tomatoes, pepper, and cook for 15 minutes.
4. Stir in capers, olives, and mix until well blended. Then add the spices, and cook for 5 minutes.
5. Add the remaining butter and cook for 10 minutes.
6. Add the cheese, and mix it with the cooked pasta.

Serve with grated Parmesan or Romano!

Quick and Easy Chicken Soup

I think that just about everyone loves chicken soup, sometimes in this busy world, we don't have time to make it the traditional way. This recipe is quick and delicious! I make it with pasta instead of potatoes. Use any size of pasta. I like smaller sizes like ditalini or elbow. Cook the pasta separately because when you cook the pasta in the broth, it absorbs a lot of the broth.

Ingredients:

1 pound chicken tenders
1/2 cup chopped celery
1/2 cup chopped onion
1 32-ounce carton chicken broth
2 cups water
1 teaspoon salt
1/2 teaspoon pepper
1 tablespoon Better Than Bouillon chicken base
1 cup baby carrots
1/2 cup uncooked pasta
1 tablespoon vegetable oil

Directions:

1. In a Dutch oven, add the tenders, celery, onion, chicken broth, water, chicken base, salt, and pepper.
2. Bring to a boil, reduce heat, and simmer for 30 minutes or until chicken is cooked through.
3. Add carrots, and cook for 15 minutes more.
4. Cook the pasta, drain separately, put it back in the pan, and toss the pasta with the oil (the oil keeps it from sticking together).
5. Put some of the pasta in each bowl, and ladle the soup on top.

Roasted Chicken

I love roasted chicken even better than roasted turkey. I use the carcass with any leftover meat and make chicken soup. The carcass gives it so much flavor from roasting the chicken and all the delicious seasonings.

Ingredients:

> 1 whole 3-pound chicken with giblets removed
> 1 stalk celery with leaves cut in half
> 1 whole small onion, peeled
> 1 whole clove garlic, peeled
> 1 teaspoon salt
> 1/2 teaspoon pepper
> 1/2 teaspoon dried thyme
> 1/2 teaspoon dried rosemary
> 1 tablespoon olive oil

Directions:

1. Preheat the oven to 350 degrees.
2. Wash the chicken inside and out then pat dry.
3. Rub the inside of the chicken with 1/2 teaspoon of salt.
4. Place the celery and onion in the cavity of the chicken.
5. Rub the chicken with olive oil, and sprinkle with the remaining ingredients.
6. Place chicken in a roasting pan and roast it for 1 hour and 15 minutes or until it reaches 180 degrees.
7. Baste occasionally.

Don't throw the carcass away. We're going to make soup!

Serves 6!

Sausage and Rigatoni Parmesan

Jerry came up with this recipe. Of course, I had to do the cooking. Actually, he grills the sausage for the dish. We had a weekend with a lot of company, and there were many leftovers. I had made a marinara sauce, and we also had leftover sausage from the day before.

Ingredients:

     2 cups marinara sauce
     5 hot or mild sausage links cooked on the grill
     1 pound cooked rigatoni
     1/2 cup grated Parmesan or Romano cheese
     8 ounces shredded mozzarella cheese

Directions:

1. Preheat the oven to 350 degrees.
2. In a large mixing bowl, add the pasta, sausage, and 1 1/2 cup of the marinara sauce. Mix completely.
3. Grease a 9 × 14-inch pan, add the mixture, cover with foil, and bake for 20 minutes.
4. Top with the cheeses and return to the oven until the cheese is melted.

Serve with the leftover sauce and grated cheese!

Sausage with Rigatoni and Sun-Dried Tomatoes

This recipe is full of flavor not just from the sausage and sundried tomatoes but it also takes spinach and pignoli nuts. The roasted pignoli nuts are so delicious and pair so well especially with the sundried tomatoes. There are two ways that the sausage can be cooked (grilled or sautéed) because the oil from the sausage will not be used.

Ingredients:

> 1 pound Italian sausage (hot or sweet)
> 1 tablespoon vegetable oil
> 3 tablespoons extra-virgin olive oil
> 6 ounces fresh baby spinach
> 3 ounces sundried tomatoes
> 1/3 cup toasted pignoli nuts
> 1 teaspoon salt
> 1/4 teaspoon black pepper
> 1 pound cooked rigatoni
> 1/2 cup grated, either Romano or Parmesan

Directions:

1. Heat the vegetable oil in a sauté to medium heat, add the sausage, and brown on all sides until the sausage is cooked all the way through.
2. In another sauté pan, heat the olive oil, add the spinach, and sundried tomatoes and sauté until the spinach has slightly wilted, then add the salt and pepper.
3. Cut the sausage into 1-inch rounds and add the sausage to the pasta.
4. Mix the sundried tomatoes and spinach into the pasta.
5. Top the pasta mixture with the pignoli nuts, and sprinkle with grated cheese.

Serve with extra grated cheese!

Scalloped Potatoes and Ham

Whenever we have a spiral ham, there is always a lot of leftover ham. Sometimes we make ham and cabbage or pasta fagioli. The recipe that gets the most requested dish to use the ham for is scalloped potatoes and ham. I like to make a white sauce, which makes it creamier. Also, I cut my potatoes very thin. I like to serve it with peas and applesauce.

Ingredients:

    8 medium yellow potatoes, thinly sliced
    10 slices of ham
    1 yellow onion, sliced thinly (optional)
    3 tablespoons butter
    3 tablespoons flour
    3 cups milk
    1/2 teaspoon salt
    1/2 teaspoon pepper

Directions:

1.   Preheat the oven to 350 degrees.
2.   Grease a 9 × 14-inch glass baking dish.
3.   In a Dutch oven, melt the butter until bubbling. Add the flour, salt, and pepper. Mix together quickly.
4.   Slowly add the milk until it boils, stirring constantly. Reduce the heat and let it simmer for 1 minute. Continue stirring. Set aside.
5.   Place a layer of potatoes, then onions and ham. Continue until all the ingredients are used up.
6.   Pour the white sauce evenly over the entire baking dish.
7.   Cover with foil and bake for 1 hour, take the foil off, and broil until golden brown.

Serves many!

Scallops a la Olivia

Olivia is our youngest daughter. She is kind and very funny. Olivia is very close to her siblings. She can be silly at times, and they love to tease her. Olivia loves to cook and eat. My advice to the man in her life is to keep her fed especially if she is hangry. She truly appreciates my cooking and always encourages me to come up with new recipes. She used to be my prep cook, but I find myself prepping for her. Olivia enjoys reading cookbooks, and that is one reason she said, "Mom you need to write a cookbook." One night, we were about to cook scallops for dinner, and she wanted to come up with something original. Olivia didn't use garlic because she wanted the sweetness of the onion to flavor the scallops. This is what she came up with.

Ingredients:

> 1-pound sea scallops
> salt
> pepper
> 1 tablespoon olive oil
> 1/2 cup white wine
> 1/4 cup butter
> 1 large white onion cut into large rings

Directions:

1. Salt and pepper scallops.
2. Heat the oil in a cast-iron pan and sear the scallops until golden on both sides.
3. Take out the scallops and keep warm.
4. Add the white wine and scrape up any remaining bits.
5. Add the butter and blend with the mixture in the pan.
6. Next, add the scallops and place an onion ring around each scallop (any remaining onion put on top of the scallops).
7. Simmer for 30 minutes covered, stirring occasionally.

Serves 4!

Seafood with Fresh Tomato Sauce

This dish, also called zuppa di pesce, is perfected with a fresh tomato paste and served with either crusty bread or pasta. I have served it over homemade gnocchi or homemade ravioli. Now it's well-known that when my children that live out of town come to visit, they want me to cook or if I visit them. It has almost become a competition of who will have Mom make the most complex favorite recipes. They even send pictures to one another to show them what they are about to eat. I was visiting Vinny, Stevi, and Liliana in Utah, and Vinny wanted this dish but he also wanted homemade ravioli. He sent the pictures, including apple pie, sauce with meatballs, and Italian cookies. Honestly, we had a great time. A few months later, I went to New York to see Brian, Christina, Lorenzo, and Mark. Well, Brian wanted the same dinner which, of course, we made. I love sharing my recipes with them and showing them how to make them. There is so much bonding while cooking together. Seafood lovers are going to love this dish.

Ingredients:

   5 tomatoes, peeled, deseeded, and membranes removed
   3 whole shallots, finely chopped
   3 cloves garlic, minced
   3 tablespoons extra-virgin olive oil
   1/4 to 1/2 cup red wine vinegar
   2 sticks butter, softened
   1/2 cup parsley, chopped
   1 lemon, juiced
   1 cup white wine
   3/4 cup heavy cream
   1/2 pound sea scallops
   1/2 raw pound shrimp with the shells on
   2 dozen littleneck clams
   1 loaf baguette French bread, sliced diagonally or 1 pound pasta

Directions:

1. Core tomatoes, cut an *X* on the bottom, and one at a time. Blanch them for 30 seconds, and immediately put them in ice water to stop the cooking process.
2. Remove the skin. Continue until all of the tomatoes are peeled.

3. Cut the tomatoes into quarters. Remove the seeds and any membranes.
4. Finely chop the tomatoes.
5. Heat 1 tablespoon olive oil in a sauté pan and add the tomatoes, 1 finely chopped shallot, and 1 minced garlic glove.
6. Sauté in the pan for about 25 minutes until all liquid is absorbed.
7. Once the liquid is absorbed, add the red wine vinegar and stir until the vinegar is incorporated.
8. Remove from pan, put in a bowl, and set aside.
9. To prepare the lemon garlic butter, mix the butter, parsley, 1 minced garlic clove, and 3 tablespoons lemon juice. Place it in the refrigerator.
10. For the rest of the recipe, I use a deep stainless-steel sauté pan with a lid.
11. Prepare the seafood.
12. Scrub the clams because they may have grit on the shells.
13. Do not wash the scallops because they are like a sponge and will soak up the water instead of the sauce. Remove the shells from the shrimp, and devein.
14. Salt and pepper the scallops, put 1 tablespoon olive oil in the pan, and bring to medium heat. Add the scallops, 1 finely chopped shallot, and 1 minced clove garlic. Sauté until brown on both sides. Remove and keep warm.
15. Add 1/2 cup wine and deglaze the pan. Add the shrimp, and cook until pink. Remove and keep warm.
16. Add 1 tablespoon olive oil, the other 1/2 cup of wine, 1 minced clove garlic, 1 finely chopped shallot, and add the clams. Cook the clams until opened, remove, and keep warm.
17. Add the tomato paste to the pan and stir in the butter until the 2 are completely blended together. Add the heavy cream and blend with the mixture.
18. Add the seafood to the sauce until warm. I put the lid on and warm the seafood for about 3 minutes.
19. Transfer to a large shallow bowl, and serve.

Serve with either grated Parmesan or Romano cheese!

Shakshuka and Shawarma

My sister Chery and her husband came to visit from their home in Los Vegas. She made several different recipes, and these are two of them. My family enjoyed not only their company but also my sister's dishes; they were a real hit. Growing up, we lived in Utica, New York, for nine years. There was a Lebanese restaurant called Karats; now it is called Karam's. My sister went to school with their daughter Maryann, and they are still friends to this day. This is where my sister got her experience cooking Lebanese food and authentic recipes. She served the first recipe for breakfast; the rest were a whole dinner.

Shakshuka ingredients:

> 1 red pepper cut into 1/2-inch pieces
> 1 med onion cut into 1/2-inch pieces
> 1 28-ounce can crushed tomatoes
> 1 clove crushed garlic or 1/2 teaspoon garlic powder
> 1/2 jar mild harissa
> 6 eggs
> 1 tablespoon olive or avocado oil

Directions:

1. Heat oil in a cast-iron (or ovenproof) fry pan.
2. Sauté the peppers and onions until they begin to get tender.
3. Add crushed tomatoes, garlic, and harissa. Bring to a low boil (uncovered) for about 15 minutes or until the mixture starts to thicken.
4. Make 6 impressions in the mixture with a large spoon. Crack an egg into each impression.
5. Heat the pan to 350 degrees. Oven for about 15 minutes or until the eggs are set.
6. Garnish with parsley, and serve with pita toast.

Pita toast ingredients:

> 2 pieces pita bread, cut into triangles
> 2 tablespoons olive oil
> 1/2 teaspoon garlic salt

Directions:

1. Divide pita triangles and place pita on a baking sheet, smooth side up. Brush pita with olive oil, and sprinkle with garlic salt.
2. Bake at 350 degrees for 5 minutes.

Shawarma ingredients:

1 pound ground lamb
1 1/2 pounds ground sirloin beef
1/2 cup finely chopped onion
2 tablespoon finely chopped parsley
1 1/2 teaspoon salt
1/4 teaspoon ground black pepper
1 teaspoon ground cumin
1/2 teaspoon garlic powder

Directions:

1. Mix ingredients well with your hands. Divide into 8 large meatballs.
2. Take a meatball and form evenly onto a skewer in the shape of a hot dog or sausage. Repeat for all 8 meatballs. Place on a platter and cover. Leave at room temperature until the grill is hot.
3. Grill for about 5 minutes on each side until the meat on skewers feels firm (10 to 15 minutes total time).
4. Place meat on a platter and cover with foil for 5 to 10 minutes.
5. Serve with laban or plain yogurt.

Tabbouleh Salad

Ingredients:

- 1 bunch Italian curly parsley
- 1/2 sweet onion
- 1 pint grape tomatoes
- 3 leaves fresh mint
- 1 cup cracked wheat (bulgar)
- 2 fresh lemons, squeezed
- 2 tablespoons virgin olive oil
- 1 teaspoon salt
- 1/4 teaspoon pepper

Directions:

1. Prepare bulgar according to package and cool.
2. Wash and chop parsley, onion, tomato, and mint finely.
3. Mix with cooled bulgar.
4. Toss with lemon juice, olive oil, salt, and pepper.

Serves many!

Basmati Rice Pilaf

Ingredients:

  1 1/2 cups basmati rice
  1/2 cup broken angel hair pasta (uncooked)
  2 tablespoons oil
  3 cups chicken broth
  2 tablespoons dehydrated soup mix

Directions:

1. Rinse and drain the rice.
2. In a Dutch oven, heat the oil.
3. When the oil is hot, add the pasta, and cook till medium brown. Stir in the rice, and fry for a few minutes. Stir in chicken broth and dehydrated soup mix.
4. Cover and simmer on low for about 20 minutes. Stir before serving.

Short Ribs with a Homemade Barbecue Sauce

I had never had short ribs until my mother-in-law served them for a Sunday dinner. They were so tender and delicious! I asked her what the sauce was, and she said that she makes her own barbecue sauce. Some people like to use oxtail, which is equally delicious.

Ingredients:

2 pounds short ribs or oxtail
1 tablespoon oil
1 yellow onion, chopped
2 clove crushed garlic
1 28-ounce can crushed tomatoes
1/4 cup cider vinegar
1 1/2 water
2 teaspoons chili powder
2 tablespoons brown sugar
1 tablespoon Worcestershire sauce
1 teaspoon salt (more or less according to taste)
1/2 teaspoon pepper

Directions:

1. Preheat the oven to 325 degrees.
2. Salt and pepper ribs on both sides.
3. Heat the oil in a Dutch oven.
4. Sear ribs on both sides until browned with onion and garlic.
5. Take the meat out and set it aside.
6. Leave 1 tablespoon of the grease in the pan.
7. Add the remaining ingredients to the pan and stir until it's completely blended.
8. Bring it to a boil and stir constantly for 5 minutes.
9. Add the ribs, cover with the lid, and bake for 2 to 3 hours.

This recipe is great with mashed potatoes!

Smoked Rubbed Filets

Brian is our oldest son; he is married to Christina, and Lorenzo is their son. Brian is quite the character and loves to tease his siblings. They are a beautiful family, always willing to help people out, and they too love to cook for people. I asked him for his chicken marsala recipe, but he said that he couldn't give it out because then his siblings wouldn't come over for it! The recipe he decided to give me is delicious too. He serves it drizzled with an au poivre sauce.

Ingredients:

    4 filet mignons
    2 tablespoons ground espresso
    2 teaspoons granulated garlic
    1 teaspoon coarse sea salt
    1 teaspoon coarse black pepper
    1/2 teaspoon cayenne pepper

Directions:

1. Mix the seasonings together, and rub them on the filets. Let it set for 20 minutes.
2. Heat the coals with soaked hickory wood chips.
3. Heat a cast-iron skillet and sear the filets for 1 minute on each side.
4. Place the filets on the grill for 10 minutes on each side or until the internal temperature is 120 degrees.

Au poivre sauce ingredients:

    1 tablespoon unsalted butter
    2 small shallots, chopped fine
    2 tablespoons crushed pepper medley
    3 tablespoons brandy or cognac
    1/2 cup beef broth
    1 cup evaporated skim milk
    1 tablespoon cornstarch plus 1 teaspoon

Directions for au poivre sauce:

1. Heat a large nonstick sauté pan over medium heat.
2. When the pan is hot, add the butter. Once the butter is melted, add the shallots, sauté, stirring occasionally for 2 minutes.
3. Raise to high heat, add the pepper and the brandy to the pan, and simmer for 1 minute.
4. Add the broth, bring to a boil, and cook until the mixture is reduced to 1/3 cup, about 5 minutes.
5. In a bowl, whisk together the milk with the cornstarch.
6. Whisk the milk mixture into the pan. Whisk constantly until the sauce thickens.

Season with salt to taste!

Smoked Beef Brisket Enchiladas

One time when I was in Utah visiting Vinny and his family, one night we came up with this version of enchiladas. Vinny had smoked a beef brisket, so we decided to make smoked beef brisket enchiladas with a queso sauce. They are delicious. I even like them better than chicken enchiladas!

Ingredients for queso:

> 1 pound hot pork sausage
> 1 pound shredded smoked beef brisket
> 1 chopped yellow onion
> 1 chopped green pepper
> 1 2-pound block of Velveeta cheese
> 1 pound smoked gouda cheese
> 1 10-ounce can RO-TEL original diced tomatoes and green chilies
> 1 10-ounce can RO-TEL fire-roasted diced tomatoes with green chilies
> 1 10-ounce can cream of mushroom soup

Directions:

1. Preheat the oven to 350 degrees.
2. In a cast iron or another ovenproof Dutch oven, divide the Velveeta into 6 large pieces and cut the gouda into 1-inch cubes.
3. Add the canned ingredients with their liquid stir and then add the meats. Mix everything together.
4. Put the mixture in the oven for 40 to 45 minutes, stirring 3 to 4 times.

Ingredients for the enchiladas:

> 1 pound smoked beef brisket
> 4 green onions, sliced thinly, green parts only
> 2 8-ounce cream cheese, softened
> 1 teaspoon salt
> 1/4 teaspoon pepper
> 8 to 10 flour tortillas
> two 16-ounce cans refried beans (you may not use all the beans)

Directions:

1. Preheat the oven to 350 degrees and grease a 9 × 13-inch glass baking dish.
2. In a mixer, add the brisket, cream cheese, and green onions. Set aside.
3. Lay the tortillas out flat and spread some of the refried beans on each tortilla.
4. Divide the brisket filling between each tortilla longwise.
5. Starting with the side, fold them in, and then roll them from one end to the other.
6. Lay the enchiladas seam side down and cover them with queso sauce.
7. Cover the baking dish with foil and bake for 30 minutes or until heated through.
8. Take them out of the oven, and let them rest for 15 minutes.

Serve them with salsa, Tostitos, sour cream, and extra queso sauce!

SPIEDIES

We moved to Endicott, New York, from Syracuse, New York, when I was ten years old. It's a little town near Binghamton where Binghamton University is. Endicott was named after Endicott Johnson, the famous shoe manufacturer, and it also is where IBM started. They have an amazing sandwich called spiedies, which consists of marinated meats, such as chicken, pork, beef, lamb, or even venison. Lamb was the original meat used, which I think is the best.

Ingredients:

2 to 3 chicken breasts (or whatever meat you choose) cut into 1-inch cubes
1/3 cup olive oil
1/4 cup fresh lemon juice
1/4 cup white vinegar
2 cloves garlic, minced

1 tablespoon dried parsley
1 tablespoon dried basil
1/2 teaspoon dried oregano
1/2 teaspoon garlic salt
1/2 teaspoon salt
1/2 teaspoon cracked black pepper

Directions:

1. Place the meat in a large bowl.
2. Whisk the rest of the ingredients together to form a marinade.
3. Pour marinade into the bowl with the meat. Cover and refrigerate overnight up until 4 days.
4. Stir the mixture occasionally. The acidic nature of the marinade will chemically cook the meat partially.
5. Thread 5 or 6 cubes onto either soaked bamboo or metal skewers.
6. Grill the meat until the desired temperature except for the chicken because that has to be cooked all the way through.
7. Take a piece of Italian bread or bun, grip the meat, and pull the spiedies off the skewer.

You don't even need a plate!

Spinach Gnocchi

I have tried for years to perfect spinach gnocchi. Sometimes the stems don't break down enough, which results in inconsistent gnocchi. One Sunday, I had time to figure out the best way for making these gnocchi. I decided to eliminate the stems, so I cut the leaves off of the stem. I will warn you that it is time-consuming, but the end result is well worth the work. I usually make mine ahead and freeze them, so on the day that I'm serving them, I can concentrate on the rest of the meal. Put them in a freezer bag, then another freezer bag and an airtight container. I like to serve mine with a gorgonzola sauce, but you can use any sauce of your choice. I like to serve them with lamb lollipop chops. Dipping the lamb in the gorgonzola sauce is a perfect pair.

Ingredients:

> 24 ounces of baby spinach with stems removed
> 1-1/4 cup potato flakes
> 3/4 cup hot water
> 1 egg
> 3 cups flour
> 1 tablespoon salt

Directions:

1. Fill a stockpot with 3/4 inches of water, bring to a boil, and add the spinach for 1 to 2 minutes.
2. Drain well, pressing the spinach against the side of the colander, and then wrap the spinach leaves in a cloth kitchen towel. Squeeze out all the liquid.
3. In a food processer, put the spinach and egg together and blend together. Set aside.
4. In a glass measuring cup, put the potatoes flakes, add the water, and stir until they are the consistency of mashed potatoes. Let them cool just so they are no longer hot.
5. In a mixing bowl, add the potatoes, spinach mixture, and stir together.
6. On a clean surface, make a circle with flour, add the potato-spinach mixture, and slowly incorporate the flour until you have a soft but not sticky dough.
7. Add more flour if the dough is sticky.
8. Flour the surface that you will be making the gnocchi on.

9. Roll out 6-inch-long pieces and cut 10 pieces. At this point, you can either keep them as pillows or you can indent them.
10. In a stockpot, fill it 3/4 of the way up. Add the salt. Bring to a rolling boil.
11. Add the gnocchi, and once they come to a boil and float to the top, cook them for 1 minute.
12. Drain them, ladle the sauce over them, and mix completely.

Serves 6!
Make sure to serve them with plenty of either grated Parmesan or Romano cheese.

STEVI'S FUSILLI AND SAUSAGE

Stevi is our son Vinny's wife and the mother to our granddaughter Liliana. Stevi is one of the kindest people I have ever met. She's a great wife and mother, putting their needs in front of her own. She is very talented and creative, even opening her own business at a young age. She came up with this recipe, and it's quite inventive.

Ingredients:

    1 pound chicken, bacon, pineapple sausage, grilled and cut into rounds
    8 ounces cooked tricolored fusilli
    1/2 cup roasted chickpeas
    1 cup cooked broccoli
    1/2 cup bottled garlic sauce
    1/4 cup pepitas
    Parmesan cheese, grated

Direction:

Mix the first 5 ingredients in a serving dish. Top with pepitas and Parmesan cheese.

Serves many!

SUNDAY GRAVY WITH MIMI'S MEATBALLS

Sunday gravy is a tomato-based sauce cooked with various types of meat. You can use pork, bone-in chuck roast, sausage and, of course, meatballs. I typically use pork spare ribs, sausage, and meatballs. It originated with large families getting together on Sundays for a delicious meal of sauce, pasta, and lots of meat! It can be a heavy meal, so Sunday was a perfect day, around two o'clock. That way it gives more time to digest the rich meal. Plus, there are usually plenty of leftovers to freeze or use during the week. When my mother-in-law taught me how to make meatballs, she baked them, and I have been doing the same ever since. When our grandson Giovanni was three, I gave him a meatball before dinner, and he said, "Mimi where is the spaghetti? You can't have meatballs without spaghetti!" I agree!

Ingredients:

4 tablespoons vegetable oil
1 whole onion, peeled
5 whole cloves garlic, peeled
1 28-ounce can crushed tomatoes
1 28-ounce can tomato puree
1 6-ounce can tomato paste
1 1/2 tablespoons salt
1 1/2 teaspoons pepper
3 fresh basil leaves or 1 1/2 teaspoons
    dried basil
1 pound ground chuck

1/2 pound ground pork
1 pound Italian sausage links, hot or
    sweet
1 pound pork or beef spare ribs
1 large egg
2/3 cups Italian bread crumbs
3 tablespoons milk
1/2 teaspoon garlic powder
1/2 teaspoon black pepper
1 pound spaghetti

Directions:

1. In a Dutch oven or stockpot, heat 2 tablespoons of the oil over medium heat, put the whole onion in, brown it on one side, and then add the 3 cloves of the garlic and brown them as well.
2. Get the oil hot and add the crushed tomatoes so that when you put them in, you hear them sizzling. Stir for 2 minutes and add a can of water.
3. Let the tomato mixture boil at high heat for 10 minutes, stirring occasionally. Next, add the puree, repeating the same process, and finally the paste. Stir in the paste until it dissolves and makes a velvety sauce (boiling the tomatoes at high heat brings out the sweetness and cuts down on any bitterness).

4. Add the 1 1/2 tablespoons salt, 1 1/2 teaspoons pepper, and basil. Stir to blend completely. Continue cooking the sauce for 20 more minutes.
5. Preheat the oven to 350 degrees.
6. In a large bowl, combine the ground chuck, ground pork, bread crumbs, milk, garlic powder, and pepper until well blended.
7. On an ungreased cookie sheet, place the rolled meatballs. I compress mine together tightly to get them moist and so they don't fall apart. Put them in the oven, and cook them for about 20 minutes or until they are browned. No need to flip them.
8. In a large skillet, heat 2 tablespoons of the oil to medium heat. Add the garlic gloves, sausage, and the spare ribs. Then sear them on both sides.
9. Turn down the sauce to a simmer, add the meats and garlic from the skillet, and continue cooking for 30 minutes, stirring occasionally.
10. Take the meatballs out of the oven, let them rest for 5 minutes, and carefully remove the meatballs from the pan using a spatula—only the meatballs, none of the grease.
11. Put the meatballs into the sauce with the meats, and cook for 1 hour longer, stirring occasionally.
12. Cook the pasta, add the sauce, meat, and serve with lots of grated Romano or Parmesan cheese.

Mangi!

Sweet Tomato Sauce with Meat Logs

Some of the restaurants in Upstate New York have a sweeter sauce than most of the restaurants serve. Most of the sauces have more of a meaty salty taste, but it is definitely worth trying. Oddly enough, the ingredient that makes it sweet is applesauce. The meat logs are made with ground beef and ground pork sausage.

Ingredients:

3 cloves garlic, minced
1/4 cup olive oil
1 6-ounce can tomato paste
1 28-ounce cans crushed tomatoes
1 cup grated Parmesan cheese
1 cup sweetened applesauce
1 cup water

1 tablespoon dried basil
1 tablespoon dried parsley
2 tablespoons sugar
1 teaspoon salt
1/2 teaspoon pepper
1 pound cooked linguini

Directions:

1. Heat the oil in a Dutch oven and sauté garlic until light brown.
2. Add the tomato paste to the pan, and cook on low for 15 minutes, stirring often.
3. Add the rest of the ingredients, and cook for 45 more minutes, partially covered with the lid.
4. Add the meat logs and pour the sauce over the cooked pasta.

Meat logs ingredients:

1 pound ground chuck
1/2 pound ground Italian sausage
1 egg
2 tablespoons milk

1/2 cup Italian bread crumbs
1 teaspoon garlic powder
1/2 teaspoon pepper

Meat logs directions:

1. Preheat the oven to 350 degrees.
2. In a bowl, mix all ingredients together, and form them into logs (about 16).
3. Place them on a cookie sheet and bake until browned for about 20 minutes.
4. Add them to the sauce, and ladle the sauce over the pasta.

Serve with either grated Parmesan or Romano cheese!

VINNY'S PASTA FAGIOLI

This is the pasta fagioli that is more like a stew, and this is Vinny's version. It is the consistency of chili, but the flavor is Italian tasting. Vinny uses orecchiette or little hats; it stays al dente which is perfect for leftovers. Plus, the pasta really absorbs the sauce and all the other delicious ingredients flavors.

Ingredients:

> 5 Italian hot or sweet sausage links, cooked and sliced into round pieces
> marinara sauce (page x)
> 1 can red kidney beans, drained
> 1 can white kidney beans, drained
> 1 pound orecchiette pasta, cooked
> 1 teaspoon salt
> 1/2 teaspoon pepper
> crushed red pepper (optional)

Direction:

> Mix all the hot ingredients together and sprinkle with grated Parmesan cheese!

Vinny's White Chicken Chili

Vinny is our third son. Vinny is a big burly guy but such a gentle giant or a big teddy bear. This is his version of white chicken chili; he loves to cook and invent new ways to make recipes of his own. He is a great cook!

Ingredients:

1 tablespoon vegetable oil
1 pound boneless chicken breast, cut into bite-size pieces
1 pound hot ground Italian sausage
1 16-ounce can fire-roasted tomatoes
2 cloves minced garlic
3 fresh chopped Anaheim peppers
1 1/2 teaspoons chili powder
1 tablespoon salt

1 teaspoon pepper
Bear Creek tortilla soup mix
1 16-ounce can cannellini beans, drained
1 16-ounce can red kidney beans, drained
1 whole yellow onion
1 package Sazón seasoning
1 cup shredded extra-sharp cheddar cheese
one 12-ounce bag frozen corn, thawed

Directions:

1. In a large skillet, heat the oil. Sauté the chicken, sausage, and garlic until the meat is cooked through.
2. Meanwhile, bring 7 cups of water to a boil, whisk in the soup mix, and simmer for 15 minutes.
3. To the meat mixture, add the tomatoes, peppers, chili powder, salt, pepper, and the Sazón seasoning.
4. When the soup is done, add the meat mixture, beans, and the onion to the soup. Continue cooking for 15 minutes.
5. Add the cheese and corn, stirring until the cheese is melted.

Serve it with sour cream and tortilla chips!

Wisdom Tooth Soup

My daughter Olivia had her wisdom teeth pulled; and by the second day, she was tired of pudding, broth, and mashed potatoes. Olivia loves food. I decided to make her a beef soup using the filet mignon with vegetables. I bought the tail end of the filet so it wasn't as expensive. I didn't realize how delicious this soup would be. This recipe is so easy!

Ingredients:

  1 pound filet mignon, cut into small pieces
  1/2 cup yellow onion, chopped
  2 celery stalks with leaves, chopped
  1 tablespoon oil
  4 cups beef broth
  1 tablespoon Better than Bouillon beef base
  1 cup water
  1 cup crushed tomatoes
  1 teaspoon salt
  1/2 teaspoon pepper
  3 large carrots, peeled and sliced thinly
  3 Yukon potatoes, peeled and cut into small chunks

Directions:

  1. Salt and pepper the meat.
  2. Heat the oil in a Dutch oven and sear the meat.
  3. Add the onion and celery, and sauté for 5 minutes or until the celery is tender.
  4. Add the broth, bouillon, water, tomatoes, salt, and pepper.
  5. Simmer for 30 minutes.
  6. Add the carrots and potatoes. Cook for 1 hour more.

Serves 4!

DESSERTS

Apple Pie

My great-grandmother came up with her own version of apple pie. She tried and tried to come up with the flakiest crust while keeping the apples firm. In some areas, you just can't get firm apples. Her favorite apples to use are McIntosh and Granny Smith apples. You can still use whatever is available, but the apples may cook a little more and not stay as firm.

Ingredients:

8 McIntosh apples, peeled and cut into chunks

2 Granny Smith apples, peeled and cut into chunks

2 1/3 cups all-purpose flour

1 teaspoon salt

1/4 cup cold water

3/4 cup Crisco

1 cup sugar (less sugar can be used for a tarter pie)

1 teaspoon cinnamon

1/4 cup butter

Directions:

1. Preheat the oven to 400 degrees.
2. In a large bowl, mix together 2 cups of flour and 1 teaspoon salt.
3. In another bowl, take 1/3 cup of the flour mixture and mix it with the 1/4 cup of cold water into a paste.
4. Cut the Crisco into the rest of the flour mixture until crumbly.
5. Mix the paste into the flour Crisco mixture and form a ball.
6. Cover with wax paper, making sure that none of the dough is exposed, and put it in the refrigerator.
7. Place the apples in a large bowl.
8. In another bowl, mix the sugar, 1/3 cup of flour, and cinnamon; and toss the apples in the mixture until completely coated.
9. Coat the apples completely with the sugar mixture.
10. Cut the dough in half, roll out the bottom crust, and put it in the bottom of the pie pan.
11. Add the apples, dot with the butter, and put the top crust on it.
12. Make sure the edges are sealed and cut a few slits on the top.
13. Bake for 20 minutes, turn the heat down to 350 degrees, and cook for 30 to 45 more minutes until the crust is golden.
14. Put the pie on a cooling rack, and let it cool down.

Serve it with ice cream or cheddar cheese!

Blueberry Pie

This is my mother's recipe for blueberry pie. It takes heavy cream in the filling and really makes it rich in flavor. I like to make a lattice top for the pie, but you do not have to because the pie will turn out just as good, and you don't need a top crust.

Ingredients:

- 1 9-inch unbaked pie shell
- 4 cups blueberries, washed and drained
- 1 cup sugar
- 1 cup heavy cream
- 1/2 teaspoon cinnamon
- 4 tablespoons flour
- 1/2 teaspoon salt

Directions:

1. Preheat the oven to 350 degrees.
2. Press pie dough into a 9-inch glass pie baking dish and pinch the edges of the crust.
3. Combine the rest of the ingredients and pour into the pie shell.
4. Bake for 40 to 50 minutes, and let it cool.

Serve with vanilla ice cream or fresh whipped cream!

Chocolate Meringue Cookies

I was at a dinner party and everyone brought a dish to pass and contribute to the meal. I've always been a firm believer that elderly people have great recipes, and because they have been cooking for a long time, they have perfected their recipes. This is a recipe from a 102-year-old woman, and I have never come across this version.

Ingredients:

    3 egg whites
    1/8 teaspoon cream of tartar
    3/4 cup sugar
    1/8 teaspoon salt
    1 teaspoon vanilla
    1 cup mini chocolate chips
    1/4 cup walnuts or pecans

Directions:

1. Preheat the oven to 300 degrees
2. Beat the egg whites with cream of tartar until soft peaks.
3. Gradually add sugar, salt, and vanilla and beat until stiff peaks and the sugar is dissolved, 5 to 8 minutes.
4. Fold in chocolate chips and nuts.
5. Drop rounded teaspoons onto a greased baking sheet.
6. Bake until lightly brown, about 30 minutes.
7. Cool on baking sheets and refrigerate in an airtight container.

Makes 4 dozen!

Chocolate Peanut Butter Cheesecake

I always make my kids their favorite dinner and dessert on their birthdays. Inevitably they request this dessert.

Ingredients:

   1 3/4 cups sugar
   2 8-ounce packages cream cheese, softened
   2 tablespoons melted butter
   2 teaspoons vanilla
   1 8-ounce crunchy peanut butter
   1 pint whipped heavy cream
   1 9-inch graham cracker crust
   6-ounce chocolate chips
   2 to 3 tablespoons hot coffee

Directions:

1. Mix well sugar, cream cheese, butter, and vanilla.
2. Add peanut butter.
3. Beat the whipped cream until it peaks form.
4. Fold the whipped cream into the peanut butter mixture.
5. Press the graham cracker crust into a 10-inch springform pan, and add the peanut butter mixture.
6. Let it set for 10 minutes.
7. Freeze for 2 hours.
8. Mix chocolate chips and hot coffee until the chips have melted.
9. Put the chocolate-coffee mixture on top, and serve.

Serves many!

Concord Grape Pie

Grape pie is my very favorite pie. The flavor of the concord grapes is incredible. It almost tastes like blueberry pie but even better! My friend Linda gave me this recipe. One time our oldest son, Brian, brought Linda some concord grapes in hopes of getting some grape pie. Well, the next time he saw Linda, she said, "Brian, those grapes that you gave me made the most amazing pie!"

Ingredients:

5 cups concord grapes	1 tablespoon fresh lemon juice
1 cup of sugar	1/2 teaspoon grated lemon rind
1/3 cup flour	2 tablespoons melted butter
1/4 teaspoon salt	1 unbaked pie shell

Directions:

1. Preheat the oven to 400 degrees.
2. Slip grapes from skins. Set the skins aside.
3. In a saucepan, bring the pulp to a boil, reduce heat, and simmer for 10 minutes, stirring occasionally.
4. Strain the grapes, reserve the liquid, and add the skins.
5. In a large bowl, mix 1 cup of sugar, 1/3 cup of flour, salt, lemon juice, lemon rind, and 2 tablespoons of melted butter.
6. Add the grape mixture, and mix well.
7. Pour into unbaked pie shell and bake for 25 minutes.

Topping ingredients:

1/2 cup flour	1/4 cup butter
1/2 cup sugar	

Directions:

1. Sift the flour and sugar into a bowl, and cut in the butter until it's crumbly.
2. Sprinkle it on the pie, and bake for another 15 minutes more.

Serve with vanilla ice cream or whipped cream!

DOUBLE CHOCOLATE WALNUT BISCOTTI

These biscotti are like an Italian twist of a brownie, chocolaty and crisp. Make sure not to overcook them because instead of moist and crisp, they will become dry and hard.

Ingredients:

    2 cups flour
    1/2 cup unsweetened cocoa
    1 teaspoon baking soda
    1 teaspoon salt
    6 tablespoons melted butter
    1 cup sugar
    2 eggs
    1 cup chopped walnuts (optional)
    3/4 cup chocolate chips
    powdered (confectioners') sugar

Directions:

1. Preheat the oven to 350 degrees.
2. In a large bowl, mix together the flour, cocoa, baking soda, and salt.
3. In a mixer, mix the butter and sugar until creamy, then add the eggs.
4. Fold in the dry ingredients, then add the nuts and chocolate chips.
5. Divide the dough in half and roll into 2 logs (12 × 12).
6. Place on greased, floured cookie sheet, and sprinkle with the confectioners' sugar.
7. Bake for 35 minutes, take them out of the oven, and cool for 15 minutes.
8. Cut into diagonal slices, and bake for 10 more minutes.
9. Sprinkle with more confectioners' sugar.

Frosted Banana Bars

If you love bananas, you will really enjoy these frosted banana bars! They are the perfect marriage between banana bread and banana cake—very moist with cream cheese icing.

Ingredients:

1/2 cup butter, softened
1 1/2 cups sugar
2 eggs
1 cup sour cream
1 teaspoon vanilla

2 cups flour
1 teaspoon baking soda
1/4 teaspoon salt
2 ripe bananas, mashed

Directions:

1. Preheat the oven to 350 degrees.
2. In a mixer, beat the butter and sugar together until blended.
3. Add the eggs one at a time then the sour cream and vanilla.
4. In another bowl, mix the flour, baking soda, and salt.
5. Blend the dry and wet mixture together, then add the bananas.
6. Spread onto a greased baking sheet (15 × 10 × 1) and bake for 20 to 25 minutes.
7. Let it cool, and then frost it with the frosting recipe below.

Frosting ingredients:

1 8-ounce package cream cheese softened
1/2 cup softened butter
2 teaspoons vanilla
4 cups confectioners' sugar

Frosting directions:

1. In a mixer, blend the cream cheese, butter, and vanilla together. Then add the confectioners' sugar.
2. Frost the cooled bars, and refrigerate for 2 hours.

Store them in the refrigerator!

Italian Glazed Cookies

These delicious cookies are almost like a marriage of cake and doughnuts. They arse not overly sweet and are great with cappuccino or espresso. Our granddaughter Liliana loves these cookies and she loves helping make them.

Ingredients:

3/4 cup butter
1/3 cup sugar
3 eggs
1 teaspoon vanilla
2 tablespoons fresh orange juice
3 cups flour
1 tablespoon baking powder
16 ounces confectioners' sugar
confetti sprinkles

Directions:

1. Preheat the oven to 350 degrees.
2. Cream butter and sugar thoroughly.
3. Add eggs, vanilla, and orange juice.
4. In another bowl, combine the flour and baking powder. Gradually add to creamed mixture.
5. Knead dough on a lightly floured board for 5 minutes.
6. Using tablespoons of dough, roll to 6-inch lengths. Press ends together to form rings.
7. Let stand on ungreased cookie sheets for 15 minutes at room temperature.
8. Bake for 15 to 17 minutes or until lightly golden.
9. For the icing, blend 2-1/2 cups of confectioners' sugar with enough water to make a thin glaze.
10. Dip each hot cookie into the glaze, and sprinkle with confetti sprinkles.

Eat some while warm, and save the rest!

Italian Toast Cookies

These cookies are so good. They are not too sweet but sweet enough and go great with espresso or cappuccino! You can serve them as a dessert or eat them with your morning coffee.

Ingredients:

    3 eggs
    1/2 cup sugar
    1/4 cup oil
    1 teaspoon anise extract
    3 cups flour
    3 teaspoons baking powder
    3/4 cup slivered almonds

Directions:

1. Preheat the oven to 375 degrees.
2. Beat eggs, sugar, and oil until well blended; then add the anise.
3. In another bowl, mix the flour and baking soda then fold into the egg mixture.
4. Add the almonds and shape them into 2 loaves.
5. Bake for 20 to 25 minutes until golden.
6. Take them out and let them cool for a few minutes, and then cut them into slices.
7. Put them back on the cookie sheet, laying them on their sides for 2 minutes per side.
8. Cool them on a cookie rack.

Enjoy!

LEE'S BAKLAVA

My friend Lee has a Greek friend who owns a Greek restaurant, and she has been able to get many recipes from her. This is the best baklava that I have ever had. It's crunchy and sweet to perfection! Lee is originally from the South, and I have been able to get many Southern recipes from her like her Southern fried chicken.

Ingredients:

1 cup honey
2 cups sugar
1/2 lemon
1/2 cup water
1 pound chopped nuts (either walnuts, pecans, or almonds)
1 1/2 tablespoons nutmeg
1 1/2 tablespoons cinnamon
1 pound butter
1 16-ounce package phyllo dough, thawed

Directions:

1. In a saucepan, heat the honey, 1 cup of sugar, 1/2 lemon, and water.
2. Cook at low heat for 15 minutes, remove from heat, and let cool completely.
3. In a bowl, mix the chopped nuts, nutmeg, and cinnamon.
4. Melt the butter, and cover the bottom of a 9 × 13-inch pan with enough butter to cover the bottom.
5. Lay 10 sheets on the bottom, buttering every 2 to 3 sheets.
6. Add a layer of the nut mixture every 8 to 10 sheets.
7. Continue with the butter and nut mixture until they are both used up.
8. Cut the baklava into diamond-shaped squares.
9. Place the pan in a cold oven, and turn the oven to 250–300 degrees.
10. Bake for 2 to 3 hours or until the top is browned.
11. Remove from oven, and pour the honey mixture on top.
12. Let the baklava set, uncovered, at room temperature for 4 to 6 hours or overnight.

Top with chopped nuts or melted chocolate!

Lemon Pie with a Raspberry Topping

The lemon and the raspberry are so delicious and pair well with each other. It's a little tart, but the raspberry topping is sweet and balances out the tartness.

Ingredients:

    1 9-inch graham cracker crust
    1 10-ounce frozen raspberries in syrup, thawed
    1 tablespoon cornstarch
    3 egg yolks
    one 14-ounce can of sweet and condensed milk
    1/2 cup lemon juice
    whipped cream

Directions:

1.   Preheat the oven to 350 degrees
2.   In a saucepan, combine raspberries and cornstarch. Cook and stir until it thickens.
3.   In a bowl, beat egg yolk. Stir in the sweet condensed milk and lemon juice.
4.   Pour into crust, and bake for 8 minutes.
5.   Pour raspberry mixture, and chill for 4 hours.

Serve with a dollop of whipped cream!

Pumpkin Spice Delight

I have a friend named Debbie. She is beautiful with long auburn hair and green eyes. Of course, her real beauty is what a sweet soul she is. She had this dessert one night after a turkey dinner, and it was a nice change from pumpkin pie.

Ingredients:

    1 large can of pumpkin
    1 cup evaporated milk
    1 1/2 cups sugar
    3 eggs
    1/4 teaspoon nutmeg
    1/4 teaspoon ginger
    1/2 teaspoon salt
    1 teaspoon vanilla
    1 spice cake mix
    3/4 cup of melted butter
    3/4 cup chopped walnuts or pecans
    whipped cream

Directions:

1. Preheat the oven to 350 degrees.
2. Mix together the first 8 ingredients.
3. Pour into a 9 × 13 pan.
4. Sprinkle cake mix on the mixture, drizzle the butter, and finish by sprinkling the nuts on top.
5. Bake for 1 hour.

Serve with fresh whipped cream!

Strawberry Shortcake

The first time I had this version of strawberry shortcake was at my in-laws. I know people have made it with a sponge cake, but I never had it. In my family, we traditionally made homemade biscuits and served them with strawberries, ice cream, and whipped cream. I really enjoyed the diversity of the sponge cake; however, when I made it, I couldn't believe the work that was involved. It was well worth it! My mother-in-law used a sponge cake pan instead of two round cake pans. It keeps the sponge cake lighter and spongier in my opinion.

Ingredients:

> 6 eggs, separated
> 1/4 cup cold water
> 1 cup sugar
> 1 teaspoon lemon juice
> 1 teaspoon lemon rind
> 1 cup sifted flour
> 1/2 teaspoon cream of tartar
> 1/4 teaspoon salt
> 2 quarts sliced strawberries sprinkled with 1/2 cup sugar
> 1 quart heavy cream
> 2 tablespoons confectioners' sugar
> 1 teaspoon vanilla

Directions:

1. Preheat the oven to 325 degrees.
2. In a mixer, beat egg yolks until they are light in color, then gradually add the sugar.
3. Add the cold water, lemon juice, lemon rind, and then the flour a little at a time.
4. Pour the mixture into a large bowl. Clean the mixing bowl.
5. In the clean mixing bowl, add the egg whites, salt, and cream of tartar. Beat until it peaks form.
6. Fold the egg white mixture into the egg yolk mixture, and blend completely.
7. Pour the batter into a greased sponge cake pan, and bake for 1 hour.
8. Take the pan out of the oven and turn the pan over, resting the sides of the pan high enough so that nothing is touching the top of the cake.
9. After the cake has cooled, turn it back over and remove it carefully from the pan.

10. Cut the cake in half lengthwise and layer the bottom side with the strawberries.
11. Spread some of the whipped cream over half of the cake that has the strawberries on it.
12. Place the top piece of the cake on the bottom piece and frost the cake with the remaining whipped cream.

Whipped cream direction:

In a mixer, add the heavy cream, beat until it forms peaks, and add the confectioners' sugar a little at a time and then the vanilla.

Serve with extra strawberries!

Tristan's Smoothie

Tristan is Jaclyn and Tony's first son, and he is funny. He likes to play video games, and he is very good at it. Jaclyn is an engineer, and Tristan definitely has her skills. He went to computer camp, and I truly believe that someday he will design his own game. He really wanted to put a recipe in my book. I told him that it has to be original and this is what he came up with!

Ingredients:

    1/2 cup blueberries
    1/2 cup pineapple chunks with 1/2 cup juice reserved
    1/2 cup strawberries
    1/2 cup canned peaches
    1/2 cup yogurt of your choice
    1/2 cup whipped cream
    1 teaspoon agave or honey
    1 cup ice

Directions:

1. Add all the ingredients into a blender and blend until smooth.
2. Pour into a tumble with a lid, and refrigerate for 1 hour.

I love you, Tristan!
Enjoy!

Walnut Pepper Biscotti

What a great pairing of biscotti and pepper. It may seem different to put pepper in a biscotti, but it adds a little kick. It actually adds to the flavor but doesn't have a strong pepper taste.

Ingredients:

    1 3/4 cups flour
    1/2 teaspoon baking powder
    1/2 teaspoon baking soda
    1/8 teaspoon salt
    1 1/2 teaspoon black pepper
    1/2 cup butter
    1 cup sugar
    2 eggs
    2 teaspoons orange rind
    1/2 teaspoon vanilla
    1/4 teaspoon almond extract
    1 1/2 cups coarsely chopped walnuts, lightly toasted

Directions:

1. Sift the flour, baking powder, baking soda, and salt together in a bowl then add pepper.
2. In a mixer, cream the butter with the sugar. Then add the eggs one at a time, and beat until fluffy.
3. Add the orange rind, vanilla, almond extract, and walnuts.
4. Add the dry ingredients, and mix just till blended. Chill until the dough is firm.
5. Preheat the oven to 350 degrees.
6. Butter and flour 2 baking sheets.
7. Divide the dough into 3 parts, roll into logs (1 1/2 inch) and space 5 inches apart.
8. Bake until light brown for about 20 minutes.
9. Cool slightly, cut diagonally, and bake for 15 minutes more.

They are delicious with espresso, cappuccino, or even wine!

INDEX

Main Dishes

Desserts

About the Author

Rosebud is from Upstate New York where she lived most of her life. Being from New York, Rosebud's influence on cooking is mainly Italian food. Rosebud has many authentic recipes of her own, also from friends and family.

CPSIA information can be obtained
at www.ICGtesting.com
Printed in the USA
LVHW072037081222
734849LV00005B/121